Hopi Silver

The History and Hallmarks of Hopi Silversmithing

Margaret Nickelson Wright

University of New Mexico Press ❧ Albuquerque

To Barton, Elena, Allen and Laura,
Malinda and Christian

———

University of New Mexico Press paperback edition
published by arrangement with the author 2003
Printed in China by WKT Company, Ltd.

18 17 16 15 14 13   3 4 5 6 7 8

ISBN-13: 978-0-8263-3382-7

Originally published by Northland Publishing, ISBN 0-87358-09704

Library of Congress Cataloging-in-Publication Data

Wright, Margaret Nickelson.
  Hopi silver : the history and hallmarks of hopi silversmithing /
Margaret Nickelson Wright.— University of New Mexico Press paperback ed.
    p. cm.
  ISBN 0-8263-3382-6 (pbk. : alk. paper)
  1. Hopi silverwork.   I. Title.
  E99.H7 W74 2003
  739.2'3'0899745—dc21

———

                    2003006710

The author gratefully acknowledges the cooperation of the Museum of Northern Arizona in making available its materials and facilities.

Page iv: Silver overlay jewelry set with coral by Phil Poseyesva. Courtesy of Waddell Traders, Tempe, Arizona.

All photographs by Gene Balzer, Peter Bloomer, and Jerry Jacka, as follows, unless otherwise indicated:
Gene Balzer: 13, 16, 19, 67 (belt buckle)
Peter Bloomer: 9, 11 (bracelet and bow guard), 12, 20, 22, 23, 27, 33, 37, 40, 41, 42, 43 (both),
    44 (all), 45, 48, 63
Jerry Jacka: iv, 4, 17, 36, 47, 54, 56, 57 (both), 58, 59, 62, 64, 65, 66, 68 (both), 70, 72

Silversmiths Hallmark drawings by Barton Wright

CONTENTS

PREFACE

⇛ HOPI SILVER JEWELRY has been crafted over a period of seventy-five years, beginning just before 1900 and continuing today. By the mid-1930s some of the silversmiths had begun to mark their jewelry with a personal stamp which they referred to as a silver mark, but is commonly called a hallmark by collectors. No record was made of the marks for some years until Katharine Bartlett, Curator of History and Librarian at the Museum of Northern Arizona, began recording those available in the late 1950s. Several years later she gave her list to Barton Wright, Curator of the Museum, who added to it.

In 1965 I was asked to continue the research. In addition to making a drawing of each mark discovered, whenever possible an impression of the mark was stamped into a copper sheet to make a permanent record for the Museum of Northern Arizona archives. Much of the data was gathered through visits to Hopi smiths or their families. The balance was given by knowledgeable collectors and scholars of Hopi silverwork. Eventually a fairly complete record of Hopi hallmarks was compiled.

The original purpose of the project was to add to the Museum's arts and crafts records, since through the years innumerable collectors of Hopi silver have turned to the Museum for identification of their pieces. However, in the process of gathering specific data on the silver marks, a great deal of historical information emerged which both illuminated and enlarged the scope of the original research. It was felt the material should be made available to a larger audience and so the present form of the book was chosen. The material has been written as it was told to me. Since recollections of historical times tend to vary with the storyteller, there are likely to be other versions of some of the incidents.

Many people have helped with the compilation of information and preparation of the book. The Museum of Northern Arizona under its director, Dr. Edward B. Danson, has provided invaluable data through its collections and archives, and from its staff members. Hopi friends, Indian art dealers, collectors, and many others have generously given information and advice.

Two people have especially aided me. Katharine Bartlett assisted with the original Hopi silver project of the Museum of Northern Arizona in 1938 and has been associated with Hopi crafts for many years. She has freely given me advice and information. My husband, Barton Wright, has generously shared his extensive knowledge of Hopi people and their craftwork, as well as doing all the drawings for the Hopi hallmarks.

Doris Monthan has very ably and perceptively organized the manuscript and edited the book, for which I am deeply grateful.

—FLAGSTAFF, 1972

POSTSCRIPT

HOPI JEWELERS are now renowned worldwide. Their art is being sought in person, by phone, mail, fax, and Internet. It is indeed a thrill to realize that the craft has gone from a handful of men on isolated mesas to skilled artisans making sophisticated adornments that can be worn in the most formal settings—all in less than a hundred years!

The exceptional thing about the Hopi craftsmen is the belief in their culture that they include in their work. Of course they are producing work for sale, but often it seems to include the genuine wish of the maker for the well-being of the purchaser as he wears the piece, much as if it were a gift of a prayer feather conveying those wishes.

Many members of the same family now work at the craft, sometimes in a completely individual style for each person, and sometimes with a shared tradition. Twenty-five years ago, few women worked in silver. Today, women are actively smithing on their own, in addition to helping their husbands and other family members.

Unfortunately, there is a minus side to the popularity of Hopi silver-smithing. It is being replicated in many other nations, using Hopi designs copied from books and displays. It is then either made by hand or is machine-made in much cheaper versions. These inferior copies often end up being sold in this country to novice buyers who believe they are getting genuine Hopi pieces. Luckily, there are many reputable dealers who recognize and refuse to handle such merchandise.

As always, the Hopi craftsmen themselves, the Indian Art dealers, and the collectors have gone out of their way to be helpful to me and I thank them. A very special thanks, also, to my husband, Barton Wright, who neglected his own research to draw the hallmarks and man the computer for me.

—PHOENIX, 1998

INTRODUCTION

▣▷ THE UNIQUELY BEAUTIFUL silver jewelry made by Native Americans of the southwestern United States has been widely known and admired for the past hundred years. Though the Hopi people of northern Arizona acquired silvermaking at a later date than other tribes, they have developed a distinctive and fine quality jewelry that is equal artistically to that of any other people in the world.

From the beginning of Hopi silverwork around 1900 to the present, there have been skilled craftsmen actively producing silver jewelry. To more fully understand the development of Hopi silverwork, we will review the growth of silversmithing among their neighbors and teachers, the Zuni and Navajo, as well as a brief history of other influences prior to the twentieth century.

In prehistoric times the southwestern Indians did no metalwork (and had no domesticated animals). It took over 250 years of European contact before they had both the need for and the opportunity to learn to work with metal.

The Spaniards were the first Europeans to contact the indigenous inhabitants of the Southwest. After settling in Mexico, the explorers and colonists moved northward in the 1500s through what are now Chihuahua and Sonora, and established colonies up the Rio Grande into the north of the present state of New Mexico and the southern part of Arizona. From here they moved out to other settlements—military outposts, civil communities, and religious missions. At first, many of the Indian groups contacted did not openly object to the newcomers. Later, most of the tribes showed marked animosity toward them, which greatly diminished Spanish influence upon Indian culture.

It was many years after the Spaniards' arrival that the Native Americans acquired flocks of sheep, and horses came still later. After they obtained horses there was a greater need for metalwork because of the need for bridle bits, but the opportunity to learn to work with metal was still lacking. Arthur Woodward, in his book, *Navajo Silver: A Brief History of Navajo Silversmithing,* stresses the point that smithing could not be learned "passing by" on a raiding party. There had to be opportunity for the Indians to observe the many vital steps in the making of metal objects, and perhaps even the chance to do some of the work for themselves. They would also have to obtain the necessary tools and the metal to work with before any could begin smithing for themselves. Even if a skilled metal worker became a captive of the Indians, Woodward points out, he could not teach them his craft without tools and metal.

The first record of a Navajo blacksmith appears about 1850. This man, Atsidi Sani, or Herrero (Iron Worker) as the Mexicans called him, became a silversmith as well. In *The Navajo and Pueblo Silversmiths,* John Adair recounts the story a Navajo tells about Atsidi Sani: "He was the first Navajo to learn how to make silver, and my grandmother told me that he had learned how to work with iron before that. He learned how to do this from a Mexican by the name of Nakai Tsosi (Thin Mexican) who lived down near Mt. Taylor. He [Atsidi Sani] thought he could earn money by making bridles. In those days the Navajo bought all their bridles from the Mexicans, and Atsidi Sani thought that if he learned how to make them the Navajo would buy them from him . . ." (Adair: 4).

Referring to Atsidi, Woodward quotes from an 1865 government report: "Don't know whether the young men could repair the ploughs or not; [Herrero] is a blacksmith, and from him some of the young men have learned. Herrero Delgadito works in iron—makes bridle bits . . . " (Woodward: 24).

It is the Mexican teacher at Mt. Taylor who is most often mentioned. However, Woodward also notes that in 1853 at Ft. Defiance, Arizona, there was another Mexican silversmith working as an assistant to an American blacksmith, and that Atsidi Sani visited their forges. In an article for the Museum of New Mexico's newsletter *El Palacio*, October 1928, Frederick Webb Hodge writes of a trader on the Navajo Reservation in the 1800s who told of Mexican silversmiths coming around each year and making up silver for the Navajos in exchange for their horses. These men, who must have influenced Navajo silversmiths, are all called "Mexican" and it is likely that, to the Navajo, they were truly removed, in custom as well as time, from the hated Spanish conquerors of the past.

Metalwork was probably adopted by the Zuni Pueblo Indians of western New Mexico around 1850 at approximately the same time the Navajo began to learn the craft. Adair places the making of brass and copper jewelry at Zuni in 1830 or 1840, though he does not give his source of information. There is a drawing of a Zuni blacksmith shop (cover illustration, *El Palacio*, October 1928) in Sitgreave's report of his 1852 visit, but there is no mention of metalwork in the text. A man called Ax Maker (Kiwashinakwe) who mended axes and hoes, is called the first Zuni blacksmith (Adair: 121).

James Stevenson, collecting Zuni artifacts for the Smithsonian Institution in 1879, obtained a sandstone mold for "shaping metal into such forms as suit the fancy of the Indians for bridle and other ornaments; . . . Silver which has long been a metal of traffic among these tribes, is the one which is usually melted down for ornamental purposes. After it is taken from the mold it is beaten thin, then polished" (Stevenson 1883: 342, fig. 356). He also collected pottery crucibles "for reducing silver and copper in the manu-facture of ornaments" (Stevenson 1884: 574).

A Zuni man who spoke Navajo and was called Lan-ya-de has said that around 1872 a Navajo smith stayed with him and, in exchange for a horse, taught him to work silver. The Navajo taught him how to make dies so that he was able to make his own set of tools. In the next ten years other Zuni men who had done brass and copper work learned to work silver from him (Adair: 122–23).

Once the basic techniques of metalworking were learned and the essential tools were made, traded for, or bought, a man could increase his own skill and improve his silverwork with continued practice. The craft could also spread among others in the tribe as long as there was a demand for the jewelry. This happened among both the Zuni and Navajo, who gradually increased the output of silver jewelry for their native markets until the 1900s. Then the demands of the white tourists for Indian jewelry made many changes in the economics of silvermaking for the Zuni, whose village lay near the railroad, and for those Navajo who lived near marketing outlets.

The silverwork of both tribes was similar in appearance in the late 1800s—it was heavyweight, and when set with turquoise, only a few large stones were used. For their silver, the smiths melted down American silver coins until about 1890, when government officials became strict about defacing United States money. At that time, most of the men began to use Mexican pesos, which some of the traders kept in supply for the smiths.

Thus, at the time the Hopis acquired silversmithing, their neighbors were making massive jewelry, sometimes set with large turquoise stones, but still without individual tribal style. The Hopi smiths readily became skillful at working the metal, but as with the Navajo and Zuni, it took thirty or forty years to develop a distinctive style of silverwork.

1

HOPI CRAFTS AND CULTURE: 1500–1890

⇛ **THE HOPIS** of northeastern Arizona still live in towns they were inhabiting in the 1500s and practice a religion little changed by the white man. Their homes of stone are scattered about on the top—or just at the foot—of sheer mesa cliffs surrounded by miles of sandy desert land. From this land they harvest abundant fruit and vegetables, and particularly corn, the grain that is the center of their lives. This harvest is possible only when they fulfill their duties in the relationship with their many supernatural beings or kachinas. They still work at many crafts—pottery, basketry, and weaving—which were necessities to them in their Stone Age life before A.D. 1500 but are now thought of as beautiful art forms.

Before contact with Europeans, the Hopis did no metalwork. For cooking they used pottery and stone; for cutting tools and for farming they used stone; for fastenings they used leather, sinew, and plant fibers. Jewelry was made from bone, wood, shell, colored stones (including turquoise), and seeds.

The Hopi towns have long been picturesquely located on three high mesas in Arizona that project like fingers from the southern end of the immense Black Mesa. In the late 1800s there were three villages to the east on First Mesa. They were Walpi, Sichomovi, which was an outgrowth of Walpi, and Hano, inhabited by Tewa people from the Rio Grande in New

Mexico, who fled there after the Pueblo Rebellion of 1680. On Second Mesa there were Shungopavi, Mishongnovi, and Shipaulovi. On Third Mesa there was only the large village of Oraibi, known as the oldest continuously inhabited town in the United States because of its location at the same site from around A.D. 1150. Farthest to the west was the farming outpost of Moenkopi. At the end of the 1800s people were just beginning to move to the foot of the mesas at Polacca and Kykotsmovi (New Oraibi).

While the Hopis were much more remote from European settlements than some other Indian groups, by the 1890s there were numerous changes to be seen in their lives. They had acquired many additions to their agriculture—new vegetables and fruits, especially the peach, and flocks of sheep as well as burros and horses. Missionary efforts by various groups had met with little success until this time, when Mennonite converts were made at Oraibi. There was a Baptist mission at Mishongnovi and a Mormon colony at Moenkopi; the latter was moved out by the government in 1907. Some schooling was being enforced by the government, at times through such drastic action as tying up the men and cutting off their hair unless they sent their children to school.

The issue of cooperating with the white men caused much trouble in the village of Oraibi, along with dissension about the practice of their religious ceremonies. Bad feelings between the Conservative (those hostile to the federal government) and Progressive (those who cooperated with the government) factions in the village finally resulted in the two groups attempting to perform important religious observances in duplicate. The quarrel was resolved on September 8, 1906, when the two factions came together outside the village. The Conservative leader, Yukioma, drew a line on the ground and said that whoever pushed him over it would be the winner. All the men (the boys were not allowed to join in for fear they would be injured) pushed against one another until finally Yukioma and his followers were forced far over the line and were declared the losers. They were permitted to take such of their belongings as they could carry and had to leave that day. Bloodshed was prevented by many of the relatives who, while politically siding with the Progressive faction, were grieved to lose their close relations—sons, daughters, mothers, fathers, husbands, or wives. Age made no difference; even blind old people were led away and their houses ripped apart by the remaining villagers.

The people moved to a sandy area with a good spring, called Hotevilla, about eight miles across the mesa from Oraibi, and established a new village there. The next year some of the people wanted to move back to Oraibi but were refused, so they formed still another village at a place nearby, called Bacavi, which also had a spring.

At the end of the 1800s skilled Hopi artisans continued to produce a quantity of craft work. Metal cooking utensils had not yet replaced pottery, so it was still made by the women from all three mesas. But before too long, pottery making was to die out completely at the villages of Second Mesa, and on Third Mesa was to be represented only by undecorated culinary ware. Now the women of First Mesa are considered the only Hopi potters.

Many types of basketry were made by Hopi women. Utilitarian baskets of coarse wicker and of yucca were made in all the villages. The Oraibi women and the women who lived in the seceding Third Mesa villages were noted for flat wicker plaques made from rabbit brush dyed many colors. Women from Second Mesa specialized in coiled basketry made by wrapping a bundle of galleta grass with thin strips of yucca leaf. The bundle was coiled into a spiral and sewn together with the yucca as it was bound. Different colors of yucca were used in the sewing to make stylized designs on the resulting flat plaques.

Hopi men were especially adept at fashioning intricate masks as well as the complex religious paraphernalia for their kachina and other ceremonies. In addition they did all the weaving necessary to furnish the Hopi household with textiles. At the end of the nineteenth century the majority of Hopi women still wore traditional dresses. The religious dances required the hand-woven garments, and there was a large trade with all the Pueblos in New Mexico for the Hopi textiles.

These textiles provided the main trade goods used by Hopis to obtain the silver jewelry they wore before 1890. The Zuni and Navajo jewelry was used exclusively until close to the 1900s, when a small amount of silver jewelry was crafted by Hopi men. While the men had made jewelry from shell, turquoise, and wood, they were not experienced with metalwork.

Old-style turquoise and shell mosaic earrings inlaid on cottonwood root by Leonard Taho, Kykotsmovi, 1969.

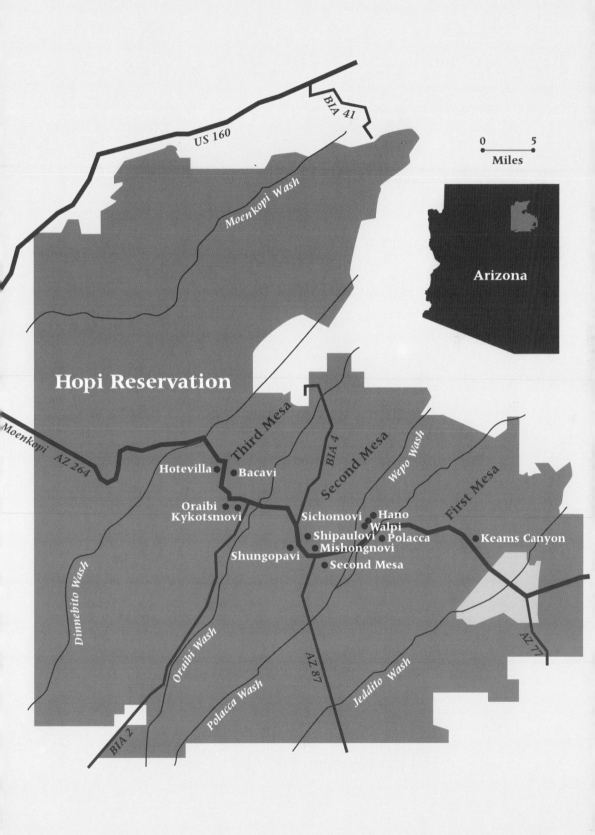

0   5
Miles

Arizona

BIA 41

US 160

Moenkopi Wash

Hopi Reservation

Moenkopi   AZ 264

Third Mesa

Second Mesa

BIA 4

Wepo Wash

First Mesa

Hotevilla   Bacavi

Oraibi
Kykotsmovi

Sichomovi   Hano
Walpi
Shipaulovi   Polacca
Mishongnovi
Shungopavi
Second Mesa

Keams Canyon

Dinnebito Wash

Oraibi Wash

AZ 87

Polacca Wash

Jeddito Wash

AZ 77

BIA 2

2

EARLY HOPI SILVERSIMTHS: 1890–1910

⇛ **In 1906,** when Hotevilla split from Oraibi, there were men from all three mesas doing silverwork. The jewelry these silversmiths have left behind shows their ability as craftsmen and a talent for design. The style reflects the general tradition of silverwork of the Indians of the Southwest during the last half of the nineteenth century, with elements drawn from Plains Indian metalwork and Spanish metal and leather work, as well as their own motifs and backgrounds.

These first Hopi smiths continued to make this style of jewelry for the next thirty years, as did new workers who learned the craft, but it was made only for Hopi use. When the smiths worked for commercial outlets the type of silver produced, as well as the style of design, was modified by economic demands. This did not intrinsically mean poor jewelry—in some cases the silverwork probably improved. But a smith called upon to make up a large quantity of less expensive bracelets in a short time obviously could not turn out work as well crafted and individually designed as a smith who made only a few bow guards and concha belts during a year. Too, the requests from tourists and traders for "Indian" designs, such as stylistic bows and arrows and thunderbirds, did not foster the use of the more subtle Indian approach to these objects, or others drawn from their own tradition.

Sikyatala (Yellow Light), ca. 1902. Photograph by Jesse H. Bratley. SMITHSONIAN INSTITUTION NATIONAL ANTHROPOLOGICAL ARCHIVES NEG. NO. 53447

Forge and smithing tools of Sikyatala, 1911. Photograph by Samuel Barrett. MILWAUKEE PUBLIC MUSEUM

In a 1939 article for the *Plateau* bulletin, Mary-Russell Colton noted that after 1890 the Zuni trader and silversmith Lanyade met with a Hopi trader, Sikyatala (which means Yellow Light: the yellow glow at sunset, the yellow of a sea of flowers in a field, the gold of a sunrise). The trading route was by foot over a trail 100 miles long. Whether they were at Hopi or Zuni, by varying accounts, Sikyatala learned from Lanyade to make silver. Since there were regular trading relations between the two tribes, the sharing of silversmithing techniques would not have been strange, especially with a Hopi man of the Mustard Clan, which had Zuni associations. Yellow Light obtained his own tools and made rings, bracelets, and hollow beads at the least (Colton: 2, 3; Adair: 173, 176). He must have learned to solder along with the other smithing skills. The photograph of his workshop at Sichomovi, taken in 1911 by Samuel Barrett, shows a permanent forge with large bellows, crucibles and ladles of several kinds, a handmade set of balances, and possibly even a draw plate for making wire (in the upper right corner of the forge), as well as a small anvil and vise (page 8). With such a permanent smithing shop, it is likely that he was able to make any of the jewelry in style at the time, including bow guards and concha belts. It is impossible to know whether he made cast jewelry, since the mold shown is used

exclusively for casting an ingot to be hammered out, though his contemporary, Duwakuku, certainly was skilled at cast

Cast bow guard of Duwakuku and a sandstone mold, date unknown.
HUNTER'S TRADING POST

jewelry sometime in his life, as evidenced by his existing pieces.

Duwakuku, the father of a modern Hano potter, Garnet Pavatea, was also a silversmith at Sichomovi. In Alexander Stephen's *Hopi Journal,* he was mentioned as belonging to a Hopi society in 1891, so he was active in the ceremonial life of the village at the same time as Yellow Light, and was also of the same Mustard Clan. He may well have been doing silverwork before 1900, and perhaps worked with Sikyatala. His cast bow guard (page 9), which is undated, shows skill both in the casting and in its inspired design.

Two Second Mesa men, Tawanimptewa and Tawahongniwa, are said to have learned how to make jewelry from Yellow Light. Tawanimptewa, described by the Hopis as a small man, did silversmithing at Grand Canyon Village for some years. In the village of Shungopavi he is recalled not as a silversmith but as the first person to put a Shalako kachina design on a coiled plaque. It seems that some of the men in Shungopavi decided that they, as well as the women, could weave coiled baskets. Several of them, including Tawanimptewa, proceeded to do just that, working at their homes rather than at the kiva. According to the Hopis, they were able to make "pretty good ones." One of Tawanimptewa's last pieces of silver, a bow guard, was made around 1930, though he lived until 1953.

Tawahongniwa had five sons who soon learned jewelry making, and his only daughter's grandson, Valjean Lomaheftewa, many years later, studied under the G. I. Bill after World War II, and became a good silversmith. Tawahongniwa and his sons were among the Second Mesa people who took part in the quarrel at Oraibi in the 1900s. After the Hotevilla people were forced to leave, United States soldiers arrested many of their men, including those from Second Mesa. Tawahongniwa was imprisoned at Florence, Arizona. His five sons, as well as Andrew Humiquaptewa, all of whom were married, were sent to Carlisle Indian School in Pennsylvania. Tawahongniwa

Lomawunu, Hopi silversmith of Second Mesa, 1911. Photograph by Samuel Barrett. MILWAUKEE PUBLIC MUSEUM

was kept in prison about a year and a half, and the others returned from Carlisle some two years later, about 1910 (Nequatewa: 1936: 74, 76, 133).

The daughter of Tawahongniwa's oldest son, Joshua, said that her father started his silverwork at Carlisle Indian School. Joshua was proficient enough to demonstrate Hopi silversmithing for a week in San Diego in 1915. He later married an Isleta woman and died in New Mexico.

There is little information about the next son, Lomawunu, who the Hopis

say died "a long time ago." But we do have Barrett's 1911 photograph of him, dressed up

Child's bow guard and bracelet by Rutherford, date unknown.

11

for the occasion, with his silver tools and a pile of coins around him. He must have died a year or so after the picture was taken. Silas Kewanwyma, the third son (called Silas Yma), made jewelry for the first Hopi Craftsman Show in Flagstaff in 1930, but died the next year.

The fourth son, Rutherford, toured the United States in 1935 and 1936 as a Hopi silversmith (page 11). Mr. W. Billingsley from Phoenix had a troupe of Hopi dancers and demonstrators, including a Hopi silversmith and a basketmaker, but no potter. They went to fairs, exhibits, and department stores—Sears Roebuck as well as others—traveling from Canada to Florida and visiting such cities as Detroit, Chicago, and Memphis. They camped out at all the places they visited, and in Washington, D.C. slept on the Mall. Rutherford, a widower, had two children who traveled with him, his daughter demonstrating coiled basketry. In Syracuse his son was run over and killed by a car. When Rutherford returned from the trip in 1936, he stopped making silver and went to live with his brother Joshua in Isleta.

Washington Talayumptewa, Tawahongniwa's fifth son, was an active smith until his death in 1963, and entered jewelry in many of the Museum of Northern Arizona Hopi Craftsmen Shows. The last year his entries were all earrings of turquoise inlay on wood, based on motifs going back to prehistoric times.

Andrew Humiquaptewa, another Shungopavi man who was sent to school at Carlisle, was a blacksmith who taught him-self silverwork. His son, Paul Saufkie, whom he instructed, was

Concha belt made by Joshua before 1934.

later to become the teacher of the World War II veterans' classes in silver-smithing, which are described in chapter 4. Paul tells that his father first worked with copper and brass, and that there was a big brass hoe made by him still in existence. Sometime after the railroad reached Williams, Arizona, Humiquaptewa would ride the train there, then walk on to meet the Havasupai to trade silver bracelets he had made for buckskins. Sometimes he would use colored bits of glass as sets in the bracelets, for turquoise was too scarce to use.

On Third Mesa, a man named Sakewyumptewa, and known as Sakwiam, told Adair that he learned silversmithing by watching Yellow Light from First Mesa, "I asked Sikyatala [Yellow Light] to make a necklace of hollow beads for me. I watched him make those beads and paid him fifteen dollars for them. I saw just how he used his tools and melted the silver. Then I tried it myself. It wasn't long before I could make simple pieces like buttons and rings. A few years later I moved from Oraibi to Hotevilla. . . . " (Adair: 176). Today Hopi people remember Sakewyumptewa by his nickname, Sió, which means *the Zuni,* "because he spent a lot of time there." It is likely that he watched various silversmiths at Zuni and, perhaps, obtained their help in perfecting his craft.

Two half-brothers, Sakhoioma and Dan Kochongva, knew how to work with silver before they left Oraibi for Hotevilla at the time of the Split in 1906. Dan, who acted as one of the leaders of the Conservative men of Hotevilla, did sil-verwork until about 1940. He died in 1972. His brother, who entered silver jewelry in the Museum of Northern Arizona's Hopi

Bracelet set with Hubbell beads by Sakhoioma prior to 1920.
MUSEUM OF NORTHERN ARIZONA

Pierce Kewanwytewa demonstrating silverwork at the 1937 Museum of Northern Arizona Hopi Craftsmen Show. MUSEUM OF NORTHERN ARIZONA

Craftsman Show as late as 1950, was awarded a prize in 1948 for an entry at Flagstaff.

Before 1906, two cousins from Oraibi began to learn silversmithing and would use it throughout their lives. Ralph Tawangyaouma and Pierce Kewanwytewa melted the solder off tin cans and used it to practice silverwork. They may have had some help with their silvermaking from Sío, who was from a related clan (Whiting: 16). Ralph moved to Hotevilla at the Split and then for many years was a full-time silversmith in Phoenix at Vaughn's and at Fred Wilson's Trading Post, and in Tucson. After his retirement, he moved back to Hotevilla where he was active in the ultra-Conservative group in the village, but still made some jewelry. Some of his pieces were of heavy silver set with large stones. The turquoise was usually good and the pieces were well proportioned (pages 16 and 36). Pierce's work was similar in appearance, though perhaps not as well finished. He did not work for a store, at least for any length of time, but continued the silversmithing part time, even after he married a Zia woman and moved to her New Mexico pueblo (page 36).

A *kik-mong-wi,* or village chief, of Oraibi was also a silversmith. Bert Fredericks acted as one of the chiefs of Oraibi from 1906 to 1910, while his brother, Tawaquaptewa, was forced to go to school in California. It was Fredericks who refused the dissatisfied settlers from Hotevilla readmission to Oraibi, and forced them to go on to form the new village of Bacavi. He had been away at school himself and was called home to help during the Oraibi disagreement. Some say he learned silverwork at school. Fredericks worked at various trades including shoe repairing but continued the jewelry making as well, and had a small shop in Flagstaff for some years before his death in the 1960s. He specialized in squash blossom necklaces and concha belts.

CLOCKWISE: *Corn, Allen Pooyama, 1948; bracelet, Grant Jenkins, pre-1935; bracelet and small pin, Morris Robinson, probably 1950s; butterfly pin, unknown; buckle, Allen Pooyama, date unknown.* KIM MESSIER
OPPOSITE: *Bracelet, probably made in the 1920s, and squash blossom necklace, 1957, by Ralph Tawangyaouma.*

1910–1940

The village of Moenkopi was a farming outpost of Oraibi near the present Tuba City. After the Oraibi-Hotevilla Split in 1906, many more people came to Moenkopi. Several of these men became excellent silversmiths. Earl Numkina started silvermaking in the 1920s and taught several younger men the craft. He quit smithing in the 1940s when his eyes went bad.

Frank Nutaima began silverwork sometime before 1920 and became very proficient in both cast and wrought silver. A concha belt of his in the Museum of Northern Arizona collections shows fine workmanship. Nutaima worked until his death in 1966.

Another smith from Moenkopi had a short but productive professional life. From before 1924 Grant Jenkins worked at shops in Phoenix, including Graves Indian Store, Skiles, and Vaughn's. Later he was employed by Browns Jewelers in Flagstaff. Before his death in 1934 or 1935, he had assisted at least two Hopi men, Morris Robinson and Randall Honwisioma, to become full-time silversmiths.

Harold Jenkins, who was Grant Jenkins' first cousin, did silverwork for about fifteen years after first receiving some instruction from his wife's brother, Frank Nutaima.

Morris Robinson (Talawytewa) was born at Oraibi, but moved to Bacavi when that village was established. He lived with his cousin Grant Jenkins in Phoenix in 1924 and learned some of the rudiments of silverwork. In the 1930s Morris went to work for Skiles Indian Store in Phoenix and in later years he worked in other shops in Phoenix and Scottsdale. At first he made plain bracelets from a strip of silver set with turquoise and decorated with stamped designs at the ends. His skill increased until he was proficient in most silvercrafting techniques. He made any form of silver that would sell, from candlesticks and bowls to all types of jewelry. To make a bowl he took a large circle of 14-gauge silver and, using an old cannonball as a form, gradually hammered the silver into shape. At first he decorated the bowls with just a simple stamped border, but his work became increasingly more intricate. He used stamp designs in many varied ways and went on to use the chisel and stamp work as embellishments on overlay work. Robinson retired in the 1960s and returned to Bacavi to help his brother

Silver set with turquoise by Morris Robinson, 1950–1960. Buckle is cast. MUSEUM OF NORTHERN ARIZONA

Necklace and bracelet by Willie Coin, late 1940s. MUSEUM OF NORTHERN ARIZONA

tend their sheep. He brought a large stock of jewelry back with him, which he gradually sold. His tools were set up at his workbench at Bacavi.

Randall Honwisioma from Mishongnovi on Second Mesa worked as a silver craftsman in Williams, Arizona, for a number of years. He first did silversmithing with Grant Jenkins at Graves Indian Store in Phoenix and moved to Williams in 1937. He was employed by Vaughn's Indian Store until 1962, when deteriorating eyesight caused his retirement. A widower, he became practically blind and lived by himself in a pretty white house in Williams until his death.

A resident of Hotevilla since its establishment in 1906, Gene Nuvahoioma worked with silver for many years. His two sons, Rex and Allen, learned from him, and Allen went on to become a full-time silversmith, working for many years in Tucson for the McDaniels at the Santa Rita Indian Shop. He moved to Holbrook in the early 1970s where he continued to make jewelry for sale.

Paul Saufkie of Shungopavi first worked in silver in the 1920s under the tutelage of his father, Andrew Humiquaptewa. He was a capable blacksmith who became proficient in making both cast and hammered silver. After World War II he instructed veterans' silversmithing classes. He ran a store on the outskirts of Shungopavi for a number of years and that, together with the great amount of weaving he did to provide his numerous sons with wedding robes for their wives, kept him from making much jewelry after the 1950s.

In 1930 several Hopi Indians were employed at San Gabriel, California, as actors. They portrayed Mission Indians in a play presented at the mission. In their off hours, Earl Numkina worked on his silver jewelry. His nephew, Willie Coin of Oraibi, watched awhile and then asked to be taught how to do it. He became skilled at the work and continued to practice the craft through the 1970s, when he had time. However, he was also a weaver, often busy at his loom. His work in the 1940s reflects the change in Hopi jewelry that was taking place then, even though he had no connection with the Museum of Northern Arizona silver project or the veterans' classes.

In the late 1930s, Frieda Santiago, a young woman from Oraibi, watched her relative, Willie Coin, work on his silver. She learned various techniques and then moved to Flagstaff, where she married a Zuni man. The two of them made Zuni-style jewelry in Flagstaff for a time and then moved elsewhere in Arizona, but continued to supply jewelry to dealers until about 1964.

An Oraibi man, Lewis Lomay (Lomayesva) learned to make silver jewelry from Ambrose Roanhorse at the Indian School in Santa Fe about 1930. He had to quit school during the Depression and went to work in Frank Patania's silver shop in Santa Fe. He smithed there for thirteen years, but then worked

Necklace detail, 1941, by Paul Saufkie.

in construction. He continued to make jewelry, often set with turquoise and coral, which had a modern look but retained some Indian character. He also did some cast work. He entered some of the major exhibitions, and in the 1971 Scottsdale National Indian Arts Exhibition won the First Award in Contemporary Jewelry. Just before his death in August 1996, he was working on pieces for the Santa Fe Indian Market. His daughter and son, Peggy and Irwin, continue his work, as does his grandson, James Rawn Lomay.

There were other Hopis who were able to do silversmithing with varying degrees of skill prior to 1940. Compared to Zuni smiths, the number was small and silverwork was a minor craft. But when the figures from about 1940 were checked for the Hopis and the Navajos, the Hopis were not so far behind their close neighbors. Ruth Underhill in *Here Come the Navajo* (1953) gives the Navajo population for 1940 as 45,000. For that same year, the Hopi population was 3,500 according to Laura Thompson and Alice Joseph in their 1944 book, *The Hopi Way.* The Navajos with 600 smiths (Adair: 17) had only about four times as many smiths per capita as the Hopis, with 12 listed silverworkers (Adair: 194). Adair's figures do not include any of the Hopis who were working full time on jewelry away from the Hopi villages, but presumably they also do not include Navajos working away from their reservation. Thus, the proportions stated above would probably be fairly accurate.

Adair suggests that one reason for the smaller number of Hopi silver-

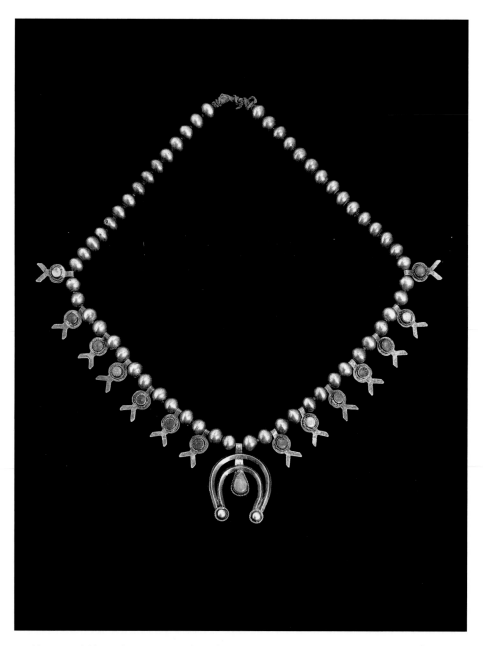

Necklace set with blue and green turquoise by Arthur Masawytewa, ca. 1935.

smiths, compared to Zuni, was the lack of economic help furnished by nearby traders. At Zuni these traders provided silver and tools on credit and bought the finished jewelry (Adair: 178). At Hopi villages the non-Indian traders did nothing to encourage silvermaking and Hopi storekeepers did not have the finances necessary to supply materials and tools on credit.

Another reason for silver remaining a minor craft among the Hopi for years was the competition of other craft work. The women continued their prehistoric craft of making pottery and several types of basketry. The men at certain times carved kachina dolls and worked on ceremonial objects, as they did at Zuni. But the majority of Hopi men did, and many still do, some type of weaving, and any spare hours were devoted to that. This was the source of the *manta* so often mentioned as being traded to the Zuni. Hopi textiles, coarse white cotton lengths used by the Hopi and other Pueblos for kilts, sashes, and shawls, as well as black wool pieces used for dresses, shirts, and kilts, were much in demand at one time by Indians all over the Southwest, and even today are traded to the Pueblo Indians of the Rio Grande. The Hopi seem to have been the main source of supply, even though the Zuni and other Pueblo Indians did some weaving. The Navajo men, however, had no such craft to compete with silverworking for their spare time.

One misconception that has arisen about Hopi silver prior to 1940 is that nothing but small articles such as rings, bracelets, and buttons were made. Actually, Adair, from fieldwork done in 1938 and written up in 1940, says that "the little silver these Hopi make *today* is for the most part small pieces—rings, bracelets, and buttons. Once in a great while a concha belt or a bow guard will be made to special order" (Adair: 177). Part of the apparent lack of early Hopi jewelry lies in the fact that it was not distinct in style from the Navajo and so was considered as Navajo once it was removed in distance from its maker. From the pre-1940 silver that is known to be Hopi, I believe that some of the Hopis were excellent silversmiths, able to work with their metal in varying techniques, and that they produced proportionately as many of the larger pieces such as bow guards, concha belts, and necklaces, as their Navajo counterparts. However, there is little indication that they made silver for saddle and bridle decoration.

The concha belts were similar in style to those of the Navajo at that time. The bow guards were either hammered or cast, and might show a stylistic difference from those made by the Navajo if it were possible to see a number of them together. Necklaces were often made of silver beads with a pendant in the center and eccentric or irregular beads placed around the front of the neck after the fashion of the squash blossom necklace (pages 16 and 23).

3

SILVERSMITHING TOOLS

▤▷ TOOLS WERE A VITAL FACTOR in the adoption of silversmithing by the Hopi. The few tools needed for pottery are easily handmade. Kachina dolls can be carved with only a pocketknife, though a rasp speeds up the work. Baskets take a knife and a punch or an awl. But to work any kind of metal requires a source of forced draft (bellows), an anvil, hammers, and depending upon the type of work to be produced, various tools for holding the metal, for smoothing and shaping the silver, for stamping the designs on the metal, and for heating the solder. The stamped designs found on so much of the southwestern jewelry from the 1900s onward would not have been possible without very fine files to make the designs on the heads of the dies.

The early Indian artisans became skilled at using simple tools and handling their metal in some ways that the modern smiths cannot duplicate. To make a piece of hammered jewelry, the smith took metal coins and melted them into a small ingot. Then the ingot was hand-hammered and annealed into an even flat sheet, from which the bracelet, pin, concha, or other object was fashioned. Later on, rollers became available for the smiths to use in flattening their silver. Now silver is bought already formed into sheets, unless it is to be used for casting. The refinements in solder and the acetylene torch with different nozzles have made it easier to do the detailed work characteristic

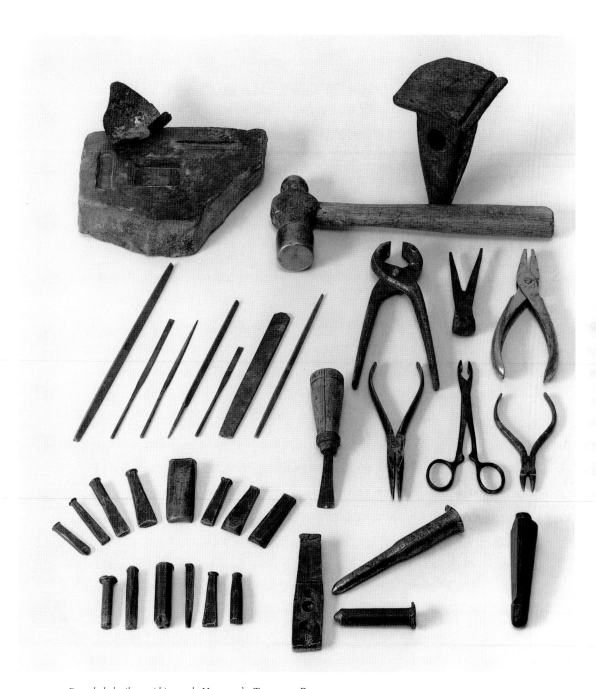

Duwakuku's silversmithing tools. HUNTER'S TRADING POST

of today's Hopi silversmith, but formerly, a skilled smith was able to do very good work with a blow pipe and bits of silver and flux for solder.

The bellows used to bring the fire to a temperature hot enough to melt the silver were handmade from buffalo hide by some of the early Navajo and Zuni smiths. A. F. Whiting, in his Hopi Crafts Survey of 1941, found that one of the old Hopi smiths at Hotevilla still had a bellows bought in the early 1900s from the Volz Trading Post. Barrett's photograph of Yellow Light's forge (page 8), as well as the picture of Lomawunu at Second Mesa (page 11), show manufactured bellows.

By 1900 there were trading posts close enough to all the Hopi towns that some blacksmithing tools were available to any of the Hopi smiths who could afford to trade for them. Part of these tools could be used for silversmithing, but a silversmith had to be able to fashion some of his own tools or buy them from someone who could make them. Adair tells of a Navajo man, John Six, who was an expert at making dies: "Die-making takes skill and requires a good deal of time. . . . The designs are cut into the ends of the pieces of scrap iron with extremely fine files, and then the dies are tempered by heating and sudden cooling in water, so that the design will hold up under the strain of hammering." He was paid a dollar and a half for a large die, and fifty cents for the smallest size (Adair: 103). Lanyade of Zuni told Adair that his Navajo teacher lived with him a year and taught him to make his own dies (Adair: 23). Morris Robinson of Bacavi said that he tempered just the outside layer or "shell" of his dies. If they were tempered too hard, they would be brittle and break off when struck by the hammer.

Since Duwakuku died in 1956, his tools (page 27) could have been obtained anytime before then. His anvil is a blacksmith's old "flatter" fastened upright (pages 8 and 11). The gripping tools include a modern-looking pair of flat-nosed pliers, and a surgical clamp. There is a pair of blacksmith's pincers, and also a bullet mold. Necessary items which are missing are metal shears or scissors, used to trim the piece of hammered silver. All of the dies are hand-made from old files or from cold chisels. The female stamp for making beads is from a scrap of iron and had been reworked into a rough chisel end. The files are manufactured, but the ingot mold is made from a piece of sandstone with a high lime content.

Today numerous stores surrounding the reservation carry any tool the silver craftsman could want, from acetylene torches with different-sized tips to the many varied fine-toothed saw blades, engraving tools, and the metals themselves. Unfortunately, the suppliers also carry stabilized turquoise (stones enhanced by various methods), as well as turquoise and other stones in the form of blocks to be shaped as one wishes. Block stones are pulverized stones of various types, combined with a binder and put under pressure to form a hard block.

With electricity now available almost everywhere, and most equipment priced so that a prudent craftsman can gradually acquire any tool needed, lack of tools no longer delimits the type of jewelry that can be made. The bracelet resting on black velvet in a jewelry shop is now the result of the craftsman's inspiration and ingenuity with no hindrance from lack of tools or materials.

Paul Saufkie at Second Mesa, 1972.

4

IMPORTANT INFLUENCES

⫸ **DR. HAROLD S. COLTON** and his wife, Mary-Russell Ferrell Colton, founders of the Museum of Northern Arizona in Flagstaff, worked to encourage the continuation of crafts among the Hopi and to maintain the quality of their work. The Coltons moved to Flagstaff in 1926 from Pennsylvania where Dr. Colton had been a professor of zoology at the University of Pennsylvania since 1909. Mrs. Colton was a recognized artist who had studied at the Philadelphia School of Design for Women. She painted prolifically and worked with the citizens of Flagstaff to foster art shows from other parts of the country and, in turn, have displays of their own art. She especially encouraged the art interests of young people. The Junior Indian Art Show was started for this purpose in 1931 among the Indian youth of northern Arizona.

In 1930 the Coltons established the annual Hopi Craftsman Exhibit at the Museum of Northern Arizona to provide a place for Hopi craft work to be shown and sold, and to furnish an incentive for excellence in the work. They took many trips to the Hopi villages to encourage the production of high quality craft work among the artisans.

At first they concentrated on pottery, basketry, and weaving. Dr. Colton made studies of the firing temperatures of the pottery. When the women had trouble with their black paint rubbing off the pots, the Coltons helped experiment with the varying proportions of ground mineral and plant juice that made an adhesive black. Mrs. Colton also encouraged the women in their use of the old native dyes for their baskets, rather than the aniline dyes from the store. The Museum of Northern Arizona bought indigo, which the Hopis had been using since Spanish times, and furnished it at cost to the weavers who were no longer able to buy it from the traders.

Then in 1938, the Coltons turned their interest to silver work. At about this time, the Bureau of Indian Affairs under Commissioner John Collier was sponsoring projects through their Indian Arts and Crafts Board to maintain and improve craft work, including silversmithing, among many Indian groups. Some of these projects had no appreciable long-range success, but others resulted in sustaining crafts that might have been lost completely, while still others raised the quality and increased the output of the crafts. The Navajo Arts and Crafts Guild was a direct result of one of the projects.

Mrs. Colton states some of her thoughts in a letter dated December 5, 1938 to Kenneth Chapman, then with the Laboratory of Anthropology, Santa Fe, and a Special Consultant to the Indian Arts and Crafts Board:

> . . . *There is only one way to make Hopi silversmithing worthwhile, it must be <u>different</u> from any other Indian silversmithing. They must produce <u>Hopi silver</u>, not Navajo, Pueblo, or Zuñi. It must be absolutely unique and of course, the supply will always be limited, therefore, if we can create a worthy product, using <u>only</u> Hopi <u>design</u> and advertise it well, we might in time create a small worthwhile market . . .*
>
> *In order to help the Hopi silversmiths to visualize our idea of Hopi design and to show them how to make use of and adopt pottery, basketry, and textile design to various silver techniques already practiced, we have created a number of plates done in opaque water*

*color on gray paper. . . . After we start the idea with our designs, we
hope that in a short time the idea will take hold and they will no longer
be needed. Wherever possible, in making these designs, we have used the
stamps already in possession of the smiths . . .*

*I would like to have your opinion of our plans; of course I real-
ize that all this is going to take a long time as I have acquired much
experience after 10 years of work with the Hopi. . . .*

Virgil Hubert, Assistant Curator of Art at the Museum of Northern
Arizona, created the jewelry designs mentioned in Mrs. Colton's letter. The
designs required the use of many silver techniques: filing, stamping, cut-out,
and appliqué. As Hubert worked, he found that the basketry and pottery
designs lent themselves especially well to the appliqué technique, though he
hadn't seen any jewelry made in that way. In a personal interview with
Hubert, he stated that, contrary to some accounts, he did not make up any of
the designs into jewelry.

Eighteen Hopi silversmiths, on the reservation and off—in Arizona,
New Mexico, and California—were sent this letter by Mrs. Colton in the
spring of 1939:

*In the name of the Museum of Northern Arizona I am writing to
all Hopi silversmiths to tell them of our plan to improve Hopi silver
and to assist Hopi smiths.*

*For a number of years, now I have heard Hopi smiths complain-
ing about the low prices which they receive for their work, and of
course, it is the same with all the other Indian silversmiths.*

*This condition, as you know, is caused by the great amount of
<u>machine made, imitation Indian Silver,</u> which is now being manufac-
tured all over the west. There is so much of this imitation stuff on the
market and it can be sold so cheaply, that the Indian smith cannot get a*

fair price for his genuine <u>hand</u> <u>made</u> silver.

The tourist does not know that difference between the <u>genuine</u> <u>hand</u> <u>made</u> and the <u>machine</u> <u>made</u> and so they are often misled, but they would like to have some guarantee, that the silver which they buy is really hand made.

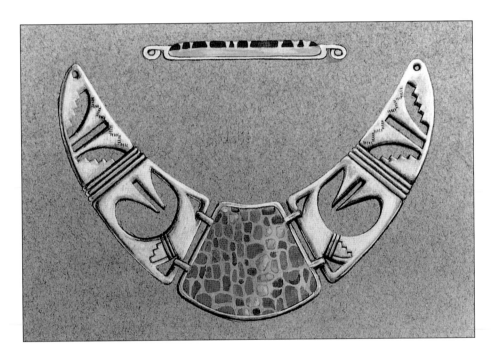

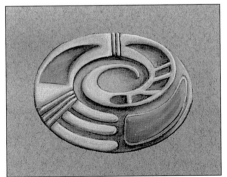

Virgil Hubert silver designs. MUSEUM OF NORTHERN ARIZONA

The government has no law to forbid the making of <u>imitation Indian silver,</u> but it has thought out a way to <u>mark</u> all hand made Indian silver so that people will know that it is genuine and thus a better price can be charged by the silversmiths for stamped pieces.

I am sending you the papers from the government "Arts and Crafts Board," [Appendix 2] that will tell you just what you have to do to get their mark on your silver work.

The Museum has no connection whatever with the government but feels that it would be an advantage to Hopi smiths to get this stamp. It is hoped that Hopi smiths when using their own designs will place their <u>personal</u> marks on their silver also.

I have talked with all the Hopi silversmiths that I can find, both on and off the reservation and explained this to them.

This is what the government is doing to help, now I am going to give you <u>the Museum's</u> idea of what should be done to help the Hopi smiths.

Navajo silver, Hopi and Pueblo silver, is very much alike, most people cannot tell the difference. Hopi silver should be entirely different from all other Indian silver, it should be <u>Hopi</u> silver, using only Hopi designs.

Hopi designs are very beautiful and very different from Navajo designs, and they will make beautiful silver and will sell well because the supply will always be limited in quantity.

The Museum proposes to help the Hopi silver smiths in this way. First, we are making a set of designs for silver, using certain Hopi designs in a new way; rings, bracelets, necklaces, etc. An order for one of these pieces and the design from which it is to be made, will be sent to each smith who believes in the idea and wishes to work with us. These *pieces will be displayed in the Museum and we will advertise the idea.*

We hope that these designs will help the Hopi smiths to understand what we mean by asking them to use one of the Hopi designs, which has not been used for silver before, and that they will then begin to make their own Hopi designs.

When I have gotten together a number of silver pieces made with Hopi design and according to the rules of the Arts and Crafts Board, then the government man will come to the Museum and put the stamp of the "Arts and Crafts Board" on the silver.

This is a very long letter and it is hard to explain, but I am anxious to have you understand.

Let me know if you are interested and wish to have an order to make a piece such as I have described to you. Thanking you, I am

> *Very sincerely,*
> *Mary-Russell F. Colton*
> CURATOR OF ART AND ETHNOLOGY

The reaction of the smiths who received the letter was varied. Several of them made acceptable pieces for the Hopi Craftsman Show that year. The delicate work necessary to make some of the designs gave a number of the men problems, and a few needed finer tools than they had for the cutting and soldering. One difficulty that arose with the full-time silversmiths as well as with their employers was the Indian Arts and Crafts Board's requirements that only slug silver and hand-polished turquoise be used. If not cast, the silver had to be hand-hammered to the desired thickness; no sheet silver was allowed. Mrs. Colton felt this could be resolved by making "premium" pieces which could be stamped by the Arts and Crafts Board and, if necessary for economic reasons, then sheet silver could be used for

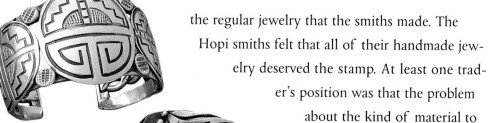

the regular jewelry that the smiths made. The Hopi smiths felt that all of their handmade jewelry deserved the stamp. At least one trader's position was that the problem about the kind of material to be used would settle itself, and that it was unfortunate to combine that requirement with the introduction of distinctive Hopi designs.

The points of disagreement would have been resolved in time. Katharine Bartlett of the Museum of Northern Arizona told of one dealer who had not been favorable to the project

Bracelets, CLOCKWISE FROM TOP: *Ralph Tawangyaouma, 1930s; unknown, 1940s; Paul Saufkie, 1940s. Ring, Pierce Kewanwytewa, 1940s.*

at first, but in the fall of 1941 came to Flagstaff and spent some time at the museum discussing the project with the staff (Whiting 4: 12).

Paul Saufkie made several of the suggested designs very successfully. A California craft teacher, Glen Lukens, gave Paul several suggestions about the new silver solder that had been developed for use on aircraft as well as formulas for oxidizing the background silver in different shades (platinum gray or blue-black). Randall Honwisioma and Washington Talayumptewa also completed suitable pieces. Saufkie and Randall Honwisioma were working on designs of their own in a similar style in 1941 (page 22) and Morris Robinson (Talawytewa) had become interested by December of 1941 (Whiting 4: 7, 12).

In another letter to Kenneth Chapman, Mrs. Colton says, "Some very nice pieces are beginning to come in now and I think that in a few years we may be able to make considerable impression."

However, the Coltons did not have the few years needed. After the Pearl Harbor attack in 1941, many aspects of business and daily life were quickly changed. The Hopi in the villages were more insulated against these changes

Cast buckle set with turquoise by Paul Saufkie, 1949. MUSEUM OF NORTHERN ARIZONA

than the average American. However, they were still affected—their eligible men joined the armed forces or were imprisoned as conscientious objectors; others did war work of various kinds. Villagers at home had to do the extra work of those taken away. There were shortages of all kinds: rationing of shoes, sugar, gasoline, meat, butter, tires. No metal of any kind was available. The Museum of Northern Arizona was shorthanded and lacked gasoline, but was able to make one collecting trip and hold a Hopi Craftsman Show in 1942. Then no more were held until the summer of 1947. During those five years it had been impossible to continue the silver project.

VETERANS' SILVERSMITHING CLASSES: 1947–1951

In the late summer of 1946, as reported in the August 22 issue of the *Arizona Sun,* Fred Kabotie and other villagers got together an exhibit of Hopi crafts to be shown during the Snake Dance at Shungopavi. Willard Beatty, Director of Indian Education, who knew of the previous encouragement of the craftsmen by the Museum of Northern Arizona, attended the exhibit. The next day he met with Kabotie and Paul Saufkie and arranged for the G.I. training program for veterans to sponsor an eighteen-month silversmithing course for Hopi servicemen. This program paid for the cost of the training, provided the necessary tools, and paid living expenses for the veteran and his family.

The classes started in February of 1947. Paul Saufkie was hired as the technical instructor and Fred Kabotie, along with his job as an art teacher at Hopi High School in Kykotsmovi, was the design instructor. The classes first met at Hopi High School but were later moved to a Quonset hut nearby. While the designs suggested by the Museum of Northern Arizona were used by the trainees, there was also a wealth of new designs taken from the large variety available in Hopi culture. In addition, the book of Mimbres designs

TOP: *Veteran's class at the Hopi High School, 1949, studies Hopi designs.* STANDING: *Fred Kabotie, Paul Saufkie, Herbert Komayouse, Arthur Yowtewa.* SEATED: *(face visible) Bert Puhuyestiwa.* HOPI CULTURAL CENTER

BOTTOM, LEFT TO RIGHT: *Arthur Yowytewa, Harold Koruh, Bert Puhuyestiwa, Orville Talayumptewa, Paul Saufkie, Fred Kabotie, Herbert Komayouse.* HOPI CULTURAL CENTER

prepared by Fred Kabotie under a Guggenheim fellowship provided further inspiration.

The silver was worked with many techniques but one was developed that is now thought of as especially Hopi. Some of the Museum of Northern Arizona designs had been formed by appliqué, in which a design is cut out and put on a base. While this was used somewhat, soon "the piece that was left" became the design, originating the jewelry technique so widely used now and called "overlay."

Bracelets by Lawrence Saufkie, 1966. Left bracelet is overlay. Right is appliqué. MUSEUM OF NORTHERN ARIZONA

SILVER OVERLAY TECHNIQUE

Overlay, as used in Hopi silverwork, is basically a piece of silver with a design cut out of it—a negative design. An everyday example of this would be the hole left in a piece of dough by a cookie cutter: if one is making star-shaped cookies, a star-shaped hole remains in the dough that is left. This is the principle of the overlay technique—the silver that is left after the design has been cut out of it is the part used. This piece is soldered onto a sheet of plain silver and the inside of the design oxidized to show up black against the polished silver.

The smiths work from sheet silver and most trace their designs from metal templates they have already cut out (a). A hole is punched in the silver part to be cut out, and a tiny saw blade is inserted. Then the design is carefully sawed out, the most painstaking step in the whole process (b). The lines must be steady and smooth, for no correction of them is possible. After the design piece is sawed, it is well coated with a flux, as is the plain piece of silver. Bits of solder are placed on the base layer, the top one is laid on, and the two are heated to a red glow with an acetylene torch. The solder flows between the two pieces, firmly soldering them together (c).

a. Tracing the design.

After the piece of silver is cooled, the matting or texturing of the design is done. Tiny chisels with ends that are straight or wedge-shaped are used with a rawhide hammer. The chisel marks are placed to follow the shape of the design (d). At this time the bottom piece of silver must be trimmed and the whole piece hammered to its finished shape, whether it is a bracelet, a pendant with a soft swell to it, or the conchas of a belt curved to fit around the waist. Then any findings necessary, such as earring and cuff link fastenings, the pin for a pendant, or the loop for a belt buckle, are soldered on.

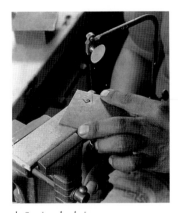

b. Sawing the design.

The piece is blanched in acid to remove any discolorations, especially from the heating.

c. Soldering design to backing..

d. Texturing the background.

e. Filing to remove discoloration.

f. Buffing

Then liver of sulfur, in some form, is applied to the interior of the design to oxidize (darken) it. This dark oxidized area is "set" by immersing the piece in boiling water. The jewelry is filed and polished with emery paper to remove discoloration and roughness (e). This is a step that must be done carefully and thoroughly to ensure a well-finished piece. It is then cleaned with ammonia water, after which it is buffed and polished and ready for sale (f).

This overlay method has changed very little from past years, except for the present consistent use of matting in the design. In 1949 the matting was seldom done though texturing was used as a major part of the design.

The students worked with copper for practice because it was less expensive, and produced a few pieces for sale, such as Tom Humiyestiwa's copper bowl on the next page. After the Hopi Guild had been established, its 1950 catalog listed silver jewelry with copper inlay as being available through orders, though Fred Kabotie said it was difficult to make because of the difference in the melting points of the metals. J. H. McGibbeny's article in the July 1950 *Arizona Highways* shows hollowware made with a partial copper exterior, but apparently very few of these mixed copper and silver items were made.

Some of the finished pieces from the veterans' silver class were displayed and sold at the Indian Craft Shop of the Department of Interior, Washington, D.C., in December 1948. The first complete display of the work was offered for sale in July 1949 at the Hopi Craftsman Exhibit of the Museum of Northern Arizona.

The inspiration of the individual craftsmen and the way they used their designs resulted in a diversity of jewelry styles. There were numerous examples of the overlay technique (page 44, bottom). Others used various textures or repoussé to obtain pleasing effects (page 44, top). Abstract forms were used in cut-out styles (page 48) while the original die and chisel technique was used for beautiful new pieces as was cast work. A fair amount of turquoise was featured, sometimes as an element of the design.

The first veterans' class graduated in 1949. The subsistence payments to the men stopped at graduation, and they lacked any means of getting more silver to make into jewelry.

TOP: *Copper bowl by Tom Humiyestiwa, 1949.* MUSEUM OF NORTHERN ARIZONA
BOTTOM: *Box by Clarence Lomayestewa, 1949, an example of texturing.* MUSEUM OF NORTHERN ARIZONA

Bracelets, 1949. LEFT: *Dean Siwingyumptewa; note the texturing.* MUSEUM OF NORTHERN ARIZONA. RIGHT: *Valjean Joshevema; repoussé.* KATHARINE BARTLETT

HOPI SILVERCRAFT COOPERATIVE GUILD

With the help and encouragement of the Indian Arts and Crafts Board and the Hopi Government Agency, the Hopi Silvercraft Guild was formed in 1949. Its purpose was: "To produce, purchase, and sell handcrafts and to operate related activities." Through this organization the smiths were able to borrow $5,000 from the government to purchase supplies and equipment. The guild members continued to work in part of the Quonset hut and, after the second veterans' class had graduated on January 1, 1951, they were able to use the whole building. Fred Kabotie was elected

Examples of the overlay technique on bracelets, 1949. TOP: *Paul Saufkie;* BOTTOM: *Herbert Komayouse.*

secretary-treasurer and served in that position until he was transferred by the government from Indian Education to work under the Indian Arts and Crafts Board as manager of the guild. His wife, Alice, was then elected secretary-treasurer, and both continued to serve the guild for many years. In 1971 Kabotie retired as manager, but remained active in the guild.

Fred Kabotie in the Hopi Silvercraft Cooperative Guild salesroom, 1972.

In 1962 ground was broken for a new guild building a mile northwest of the entrance to Shungopavi. There was some controversy at first about this use of the land. Mishongnovi and Shipaulovi villages laid claim to the land, as did Shungopavi. The land was outside clan holdings but was under the jurisdiction of Shungopavi because it was traversed by a kachina trail from a sacred spring to the village. The new building was erected without incident and the Hopi Cultural Center and Motel were built nearby in 1971. There is display and sales space in the guild building as well as working space.

The relationship of the silversmiths to the guild took various forms. A few of the men, mostly the older ones who had been away, had no connection with the organization. Others worked for it full time almost from the start. These men depended upon their jewelry sales or salaries received from the guild for their total income. Other smiths work at their homes for their cash income, with or without ties to the guild. Then there were various craftsmen who worked part-time at silver, a little or a lot, and they might have worked for the guild or independently. The guild supplied the silver for all jewelry made under its auspices and these pieces were marketed by the guild rather than by the individual craftsmen. However, the pieces were identified and sold as each smith's own work.

During its exisistence the guild has been very beneficial to the Hopi smiths by providing a central workshop and a stable marketing outlet. Without it, the benefits of the veterans' classes would not have had such lasting effects.

PRIVATE ENTERPRISE: HOPICRAFTS SHOP

In 1961 a silver shop was opened at Kykotsmovi by two brothers, Wayne and Emory Sekaquaptewa. They had learned silverwork in Phoenix from an excellent smith, Harry Sakyesva, who was in ill health and lived with them while Wayne was working for a radio station. The Sekaquaptewa brothers started a business, Hopi Enterprise, in Phoenix and hired another brother and Bernard Dawahoya and Eldon James as silversmiths. Peter Shelton, Jr. was hired as a designer. The business was moved to Kykotsmovi and the name was soon changed to Hopicrafts. (Note: the names of Hopicrafts, a private business, and the Hopi Silvercraft Guild are easily confused. To avoid this, I attempt to emphasize Guild when I am talking of that organization.) The Hopicrafts salesroom was moved in 1971 to the new Cultural Center at Shungopavi, though the workshop remained at Kykotsmovi.

The jewelry produced by the business was especially well-made, with close attention paid to even sawing, careful filing, and fine polishing. The smallest details of each piece, such as the silver tips on the braid of a bola tie, were as carefully made as the rest of the article. The competition of Hopicrafts caused a general upgrading of the quality of all the Hopi jewelry, which in some instances had been poorly finished and made of lighter weight silver, as well as becoming stereotyped in design. The Hopi overlay jewelry of today shows the influence of designer Peter Shelton, Jr. and others

Silver overlay by Bernard Dawahoya. Clockwise from top: Silver box, date unknown, JAMES BIALAC; bola tie, 1968; pin, 1972; pendant, 1972; belt buckle, 1985.

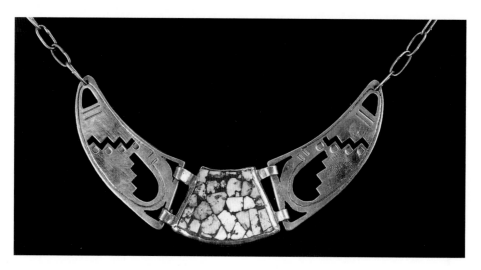

Necklace by Valjean Joshevema, 1949. MUSEUM OF NORTHERN ARIZONA

from Hopicrafts. The use of Hohokam figures, animal and human figures in motion, and elaborate detailing are all a result of Hopicrafts design.

Two other innovations were the result of the Kykotsmovi business. From the beginning the Sekaquaptewas used texturing in the matte black background of all their jewelry. Though it had been used occasionally, it now became a basic part of the design, generally following the pattern of the overlay (page 47). The attractive appearance, as well as the fact that the rough surface retains the blackening agent much better, has resulted in its widespread use by many Hopi silversmiths today. Hopicrafts also gave the final polish to the silver with steel wool, which makes a satin rather than a bright finish.

The establishment of Hopicrafts caused hard feelings for a time. This was intensified by the fact that some of the pieces of jewelry were not crafted individually but rather were made by several smiths doing the work on each piece, with each man performing one set operation. However, Hopicrafts influence resulted in an improvement in the quality of jewelry produced by all the smiths, even though at times the designs became increasingly baroque.

After the death of Wayne Sekaquaptewa in 1979, the shop remained in operation for a few years, finally closing in 1983. Many of the smiths trained at the shop continue to work and the influence of their training is seen in much of the overlay jewelry today.

CHANGES IN HOPI CULTURAL LIFE

A century has changed the world for everyone, but even more for the Hopi people. Fifty years ago the Hopi were still isolated, with dirt roads often closed by floods. There was little electricity and few phones. If people didn't want to carry water up the steep trails, or if the springs had dried up, owners of pickup trucks would haul fifty-gallon barrels of water from distant windmills for a dollar a barrel.

Today most of the villages have electricity. Those that do not have chosen not to have it. Water systems have been installed in many homes, with the exception of those at Walpi and Hotevilla. Many Hopis from First mesa live in modern homes at Polacca on the valley floor and use their mesa-top homes during kachina dances and other ceremonials. The same is true with the mesa-top homes of Mishongnovi and Shipaulovi.

Most of the food is now bought from stores at or near the villages or on regular shopping trips to supermarkets in Winslow, Holbrook, Flagstaff, or even Phoenix. Fruit trees are maintained by some farmers as well as plantings of beans, squash, and other vegetables. Numerous plots of corn of many colors are planted, not only for food, but because one must grow corn to be a true Hopi.

Corn—meal or flour—is occasionally made on a grinding stone or metate, mainly as a necessary ritual. Girls from Shungopavi grind corn this way during a four-day adolescent ceremony. But most of the corn flour used for making paper-thin piki bread is ground in electric mills at home or at a store. White corn is available for anyone to use for traditional hominy stew, or *nukwivi,* though some cooks now resort to canned hominy.

A high school for Hopi children has been built between First Mesa and Keams Canyon. Children from all the villages except Moenkopi are bussed to it, so it is no longer necessary to send teenagers away from home to boarding school for nine months of the year. Young children attend one of the five grade schools. Tuba City also has modern grade and high schools that Moenkopi children attend, along with Navajo students in the area.

Jobs held by village residents are often with the government. Many of the old people live on what they raise in their fields, plus state aid or a social security check. Both men and women work at the Hopi schools, generally as maintenance workers, cooks, bus drivers, and aides, though there are several Hopi teachers. There is other work with the highway department, Hopi police, the government hospital, and Bureau of Indian Affairs offices in Keams Canyon, and the tribal office at Kykotsmovi. A government housing project employs Indian construction workers.

Men and women who live in towns close enough to come home easily for kachina and other ceremonies work at all manner of jobs, from college professor to U.S. Forest Service employee. Most employers give their Hopi workers time off to attend any important rituals that take longer than a weekend. But the burden of maintaining daily ritual tasks falls necessarily upon the men who are residents of the villages.

For men who want to stay at the villages, who have artistic talent, and like to work with their hands, silversmithing provides an excellent occupation. It is a job that allows the men to participate fully in the ceremonial calendar, as was possible in former times when everyone was a farmer. A silversmith can set his own working hours so he can tend his fields and also take part in rituals whenever necessary.

Some smiths do not participate in the ceremonies at all, and have not lived at Hopi for many years, or perhaps ever, but are on tribal rolls, and have many relatives both in the villages and away. They may have homes at other Indian pueblos where they have married, or live in Denver, Albuquerque, Phoenix, or Flagstaff. Some have homes both in the villages and in the cities.

Ritual life is still very important for the majority of Hopis, though there are some so Christianized that they avoid contact with any of the ceremonials. Others practice both Hopi and Christian religions. The full ritual calendar has been lost at some villages, so not all the ceremonies are performed. Kachina dances continue to be numerous and the widely known, though less important, Snake Dance is still given along with other non-kachina dances.

Formerly the elders declared that anyone who "has a good heart" was welcome to observe the plaza dances. The good thoughts of the visitors combined with those of the Hopi people to make prayers for the well-being of everyone. However, some of the younger leaders have become discouraged with the use of Hopi subjects all over the country and have banned non-Indians from all ceremonies and dances. Many times it is difficult to know whether one is welcome at a village until one is there.

5

TRADITIONAL SILVERSMITHS

➣ TRADITIONAL HOPI JEWELRY today is distinctive from other Indian jewelry. The smiths themselves show many individual styles incorporating Hopi symbolism, that is sometimes easy to see and other times very subtle. There is an infinite variety of designs in the traditions of the Hopi that express associations or qualities. A woman may depict a field and clouds with rain falling in graphic form on a coiled basket. At the same time, the long fringe hanging down from the white wedding belt also depicts rain, which brings fertility. This, in turn, symbolizes a fruitful marriage to produce more Hopi people who follow in the ways of the Kachinas and harvest abundantly from the land. From their daily lives, the Hopi people are accustomed to stylization of objects, and Hopi craftwork has long made use of these stylizations. Hopi overlay silverwork is simply a transfer of these traditional artistic expressions to another medium, silver. Contrary to Indian craft work that depicts specific ideas or stories, most Hopi silverwork is designed for its appearance. The elements may represent specific things, such as warrior marks [][]; hair whorls ; an unending variety of clouds and precipitation (as may be seen in the hallmarks) ; feathers ; and whirlwinds ; but they are put together to form a pleasing effect and may be designed by the silversmith to have a personal meaning.

A prayer that the Hopi offer is that a person may live a good and long life till he is bent over with age like the cane he carries. This prayer is embodied in the bola tie made by Lawrence Saufkie (page 54). Lawrence is the son of Paul Saufkie, long-time silversmith and instructor in the World War II veterans classes in the late forties. As a boy Lawrence would sneak in and use his father's tools. Paul caught him at it, and said he would teach his son the craft. In his teens Lawrence made, among other things, copper buttons which he sold at six for a dollar and a half. After he married, he started silverwork again. His wife, the former Griselda Nuvamsa, helped him and gradually learned the whole process. She made silver for several years before using her own mark. While Lawrence may use his clan symbol, a bear, on some pieces, he has been a versatile designer and, with Griselda, has made pieces of many styles, including two- and three-dimensional Palhik' Mana bola ties and pendants.

In addition to the multitudinous numbers of stylized Hopi symbols, some prehistoric Mimbres designs have been incorporated into the jewelry, and early Hohokam figures from central Arizona are now used along with petroglyphs from northern Arizona. The designs on prehistoric Anasazi potsherds in the vicinity of the villages have also been used extensively. Katharine Bartlett of the Museum of Northern Arizona reported that in the 1950s it was possible to name the pottery type of the sherds used for the silver designs, so similar were the designs to the broken pots. Add to all of these sources the wealth of kachina figures, and it becomes apparent that there is a vast reservoir of design material from which the Hopi silversmiths may draw. The styles can range from complete realism, as in the depiction of a kachina, to a very simple abstract design. None of the many designs are traditional for use on silver as they are on basketry, weaving, and other crafts. Thus the composition of any piece of silver jewelry eventually depends upon the inspiration and artistic skill of the individual smith.

Bernard Dawahoya is a good example of this. Like Lawrence Saufkie, he

got his first training from an old-time smith, Washington Talayumptewa, and an uncle, Sidney Sekakuku. Thus he had a foundation of metal crafting that allowed him to handle the silver in many ways as opposed to just cutting out designs and soldering them. Though he was influenced by his work with Hopicrafts, his style remains his own. He will use Hohokam figures and the Hopi maze as well as other petroglyphs. He may design pieces that convey the spirit of his society with *pahos,* or prayer feathers, and then with stylized rain symbols. In addition to his fine craftsmanship and finish, he is also known for his silver bowls. As with other village men, Bernard's output varies, especially with his important ceremonial role at Shungopavi.

Forms of Hopi jewelry change more readily than do the traditional designs. This is due to economic pressures, especially from the buying public, whether these were the Hopi themselves, who were the major buyers in the early 1900s, or the present-day collectors. One of the pieces mainly for Hopi use, the bow guard, is still being made. A man who does very little silversmithing may make up one of these *maponi* for his relatives, himself, or to sell to other Hopis. The bow guards are worn in many kachina dances, as well as the butterfly, buffalo, and other non-kachina ceremonies, so they are in constant demand. Bracelets worn by the dancers are usually Navajo or Zuni, set with much turquoise, and the necklaces are of nugget turquoise or of coral.

Pieces made in the 1930s by commercial smiths ranged from bowls and candlesticks to all types of jewelry, and the same is true today. Silver styles change along with dress and home-decorating fashions. Choker-type necklaces were common in the 1940s and 1950s, then were seldom seen, but came

CLOCKWISE FROM TOP: *Belt buckle by Gracilda Saufkie, 1966; plumed serpent pin by Lawrence Saufkie, date unknown,* JAMES BIALAC; *pin by Lawrence Saufkie, date unknown,* KIM MESSIER; *Hopi rattle pendant by Lawrence Saufkie, 1968; bola tie by Lawrence Saufkie, 1970.*

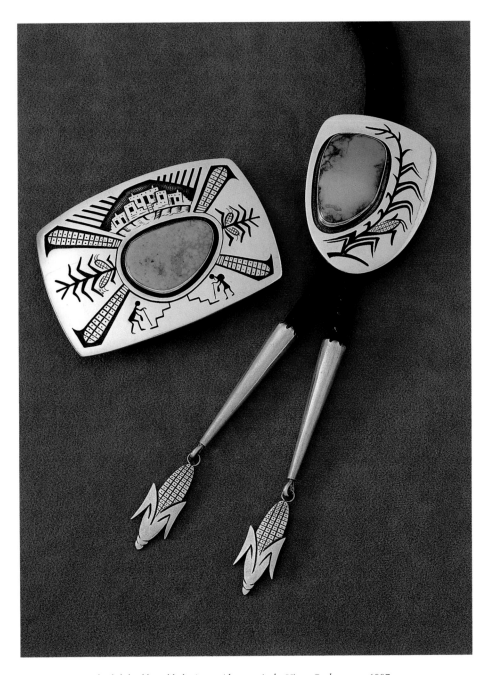

Contemporary overlay belt buckle and bola tie set with turquoise by Victor Coohwytewa, 1997.

back in the 1990s. A large number of pendants and pendant necklaces are made. Earrings readily follow fashion, being button-type or pendant, large or small, or even a dramatic single. A piece which has been in fashion for some time all over the southwest is the bola tie. It is now worn by many men, Indian as well as non-Indian, in place of the conventional tie. The Hopi make many bolas for sale, using the same type of design they put on other pieces. There are few old-style concha belts being made by Hopi silversmiths, though they do make handsome belts from various kinds of medallions.

Several traditional smiths now do much of their work in gold. Victor Coochwytewa is a long-time silversmith. He worked with Paul Saufkie before World War II, but attended the veterans' classes also. He was affiliated with the Hopi Silvercraft Guild, but marketed his silver individually as well, even selling it to Hopicraft for re-sale. In the 1950s he made silver overlay buckles and tooled leather belts in a matching design. These were unusual and very handsome. Despite an active religious role in the village and a full-time job with the highway department, Victor found time for his silverwork. Since his retirement, he has expanded his repertoire, working in gold as well as silver in his traditional designs, even using diamonds as part of his design.

Though his output is less than some of his fellow smiths, Phillip Honani continues to excel in his use of traditional symbols.

Concha belt by Bennett Kagenveama, 1991. Bracelet with Pahlik Mana design by Phillip Honani, 1996.

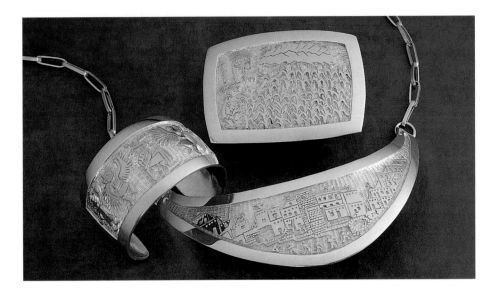

Gold on silver overlay by Watson Honanie, 1986.

The decoration of a belt buckle shows a moving line of Hopi priests rather than the Hohokam or Mexican figures so often used. And a bracelet shows a very different appearance of a mana or Hopi girl.

Philip's brother Watson is a full-time smith specializing in gold work. From intricate designs such as a whole field of corn, or an entire village, to an elegant bear with texture, his work reflects Hopi life-ways and their importance to each Hopi person, even in the craftwork he makes for sale.

While the number of active silversmiths in a given year is variable, the craft continues to be vigorous. It is an example of the great number of Hopi people with artistic ability. For a small population there are many fine silversmiths, not to mention all the other craftspeople. Aiding in this is the encouragement given to novices by their friends and relatives. Many first learned in classes or from other smiths. Then they received further training from kinsmen or kiva members. There are now many families of silversmiths, including both men and women.

Many of these smiths are using their talents along with their cultural heritage in their traditional Hopi style. Others are using their rich background and artistic abilities to craft new styles of jewelry. Both produce a vital and distinctive art form. Roy Talahaftewa and Gary Yoyokie have won top prizes on silver belts and other pieces at major craft shows with their traditional pieces.

As a young man, Roy Talahaftewa first made Hopi overlay in the Hopi guild style, learning from his brother Willie Archie, and his brother-in-law Ted Wadsworth, one of the early guild smiths. In later years, Roy shared space in

Silver overlay belt buckles designed and made by Gary and Elsie Yoyokie in 1997. The unusual patterns are formed by the innovative use of traditional designs by the Yoyokies.

Scottsdale with other smiths and developed a variety of techniques. His work ranges from the traditional silver overlay (see the pendant on the cover), to cast gold and many varieties of inlaid stones in modern abstract or stylized designs. These convey his background as an initiated, thus mature, Hopi man as well as being artistically fine. His work also is exceptionally well finished. The underside of a bracelet, though without design, is lovely to see, with simple texturing and an appliqué of his stylish hallmark.

Gary Yoyokie, from Kykotsmovi, worked at Hopicraft, sweeping and doing other chores during the summers while he was still in high school. He picked up the rudiments of silversmithing there and continued to develop his skill, finally working full time with the silver. His wife, Elsie, learned the craft from him and now they work as a team, developing their designs and making the pieces. Elsie enters some shows with her independent work and mark. The rich appearance of their belts, bracelets, bolas, and other pieces is the result of new ways of using traditional symbols combined with fine finishing on heavy gauge silver. Just when it seems impossible to use the Hopi designs another way, Gary and Elsie find one.

6

TODAY'S HOPI SILVER JEWELRY

FIFTY YEARS AGO a purchase of Hopi Jewelry would involve two choices—"Navajo style" or the first Hopi overlay made by returned World War II veterans. Today there are pieces to suit every taste and occasion: silver overlay of many styles, gold work, stone and shell, and precious gems including diamonds and rubies.

Charles Loloma was a noted craftsman from Hotevilla who worked in ceramics as well as silver. He studied ceramics at Alfred University, New York, and taught at the Institute of American Indian Arts at Santa Fe from 1962 to 1964. In 1939 he painted murals for the San Francisco Exposition under the direction of René d'Harnoncourt of the Indian Arts and Crafts Board. While living at Shungopavi in 1950 and teaching under a Whitney Foundation Fellowship, he became interested in silverwork. Later in Phoenix he often sought the advice and criticism of Fred Sharp, Bob Winston, and Morris Robinson about his jewelry. At first he did only cast work, but later in his workshop in Hotevilla he employed many different techniques in both silver and gold as his creative abilities flowered.

One jewelry technique carried from prehistoric times to the present that he used was turquoise mosaic. Examples of this type of work, inlaid on shell, wood, and even basketry, have been excavated in early archaeological sites and the Hopi continued to use it during historic times. In 1938,

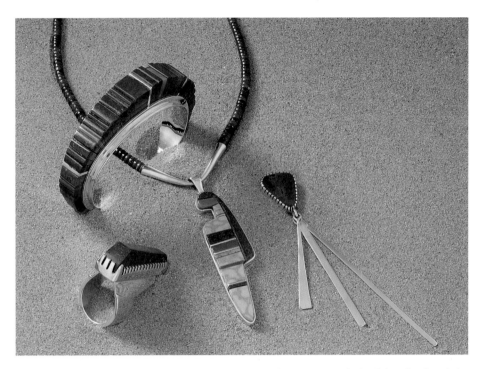

ABOVE: *Examples of the sophisticated jewelry Charles Loloma crafted, gold set or inlaid with lapiz lazuli, including a single earring, 1982.* OPPOSITE: *Jewelry in the "new Indian" style of the 1970s, by Preston Monongye.*

Virgil Hubert drew a necklace using mosaic (page 33), and necklaces of that type were made in the 1940s. At the same time that smiths were adapting the turquoise mosaic to their silver jewelry, other men continued to make jewelry the ancient way with stone and shell inlaid in wood (page 4). In 1972, Loloma incorporated mosaic in a unique way, using it to line the inside of one of his gold bracelets. In not only mosaic but in other styles he used a variety of stones as well as wood and ivory in combination with metals. His skill in design was unparalleled, and along with Preston Monongye, set an example of "new Indian" or "new Hopi" jewelry that freed younger smiths from the strictures of a traditional craft while still remaining inherently Hopi.

Preston Monongye, of California Indian descent, was adopted by a Hopi family when he was a small child and grew up in Hotevilla where he was very active in Hopi religious ceremonies. He originally learned silversmithing from a relative, Gene Nuvahoioma, in the late thirties, and first made jewelry in the style of that period. He became very proficient in the overlay technique, but then worked in a modern style using both silver and gold in many variations. A long-time dealer and connoisseur of Indian jewelry said that Monongye's knowledge and ability at working silver were unparalelled. He achieved vitality in his jewelry by the use of multiple techniques elaborated with inlays of shell and many varieties of stone. Other jewelry was made by intricate casting, often in combination with overlay, to obtain subtle pieces which

Two gold bracelets and a pendant illustrating some of the different styles Charles Loloma crafted from stone and shell. The upper bracelet is reminiscent of the cliff formations at Hopi, while the lower one is like the fine masonry in early houses. 1983.

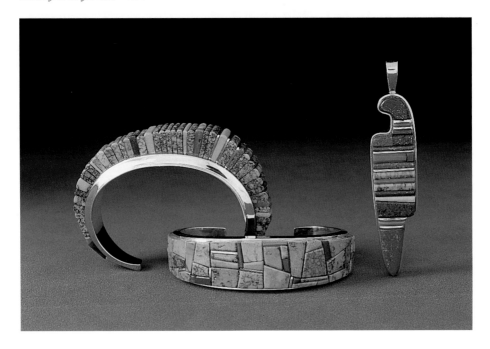

Bola ties and buckles of cast gold and silver by Sonwai (Sherian Honhongva and Verma Neqatewa). Gold bola with face inlaid with turquoise, coral, and lapiz lazuli. The silver buckle is set with fossilized ivory, turquoise, lapiz lazuli, and larulite. 1991. LOVENA OHL GALLERY, SCOTTSDALE

would be set off by only one or two pieces of turquoise. He won numerous awards in every major exhibition of the period.

Charles Loloma used various helpers in his shop, including his nieces, Verma Nequatewa and Sherian Honhongva. They excelled, and when Charles' health failed, much of the output of his shop was theirs. After his death, they worked on their own as "Sonwai." They now exhibit separately, with work that shows the influence of Loloma, but each has her own personal style.

Another niece, Dorothy Poleyma, has worked since 1989, developing an individual "look" to her jewelry.

From a different background are two Hopi brothers who have never lived on the mesas, but are producing exquisite modern pieces. Charles Supplee and his brother Don were raised in Flagstaff, but their mother was from Kykotsmovi. After graduating from school where he was noted for his artistic ability, Charles moved to Phoenix and studied under a French jeweler, Pierre Touraine. Touraine gave his students not only a knowledge of gold work, but also the ability to set precious stones. As Charles matured he used this knowledge combined with his Hopi background to craft work competitive with any in the world. He later tutored his brother Don who has become equally skilled.

Tastes in jewelry change subtly but continuously. The Supplees' jewelry

Gold, coral, and turquoise jewelry by Charles Supplee, 1985.

Belt buckle in the favorite style of the silversmith, Robert Lomadapki, 1997.

has used the traditional Southwestern settings of turquoise and coral when not set with precious stones. But they and other smiths now also use lapis lazuli, pink shell, and purple sugalite as well, so that often the pieces reflect the popular colors used by decorators of the day.

Another smith skilled in stone settings is Duayne Maktima. He and Bob Lomadapki, together with Victor Beck, a Navajo smith, worked in Flagstaff under a program sponsored by the Museum of Northern Arizona. It was designed to increase the inspiration of artistic ideas by contact with one another. Jake Brookins served as a mentor. Maktima's work varies from a magnificent silver chalice with a single inset stone to a hand-hammered two-foot-high punch ladle with granulation, reticulation, and appliqué. Other pieces are completely inlaid with many materials, including wood. His work is very bold and often is a successful incorporation of an overlay design with colorful inlay as part of the whole.

Bob Lomadapki's smithing took a different path. His work, as well as Michael Kabotie's, relies upon the strength of the design itself in silver and black. He works with heavy-gauge silver and often a single piece of turquoise. His bold

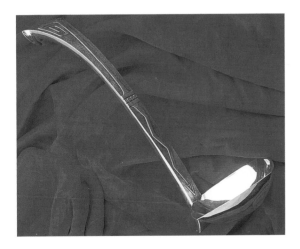

Silver ladle by Duayne Maktima, 1990. Photograph by Lisa E. Erramousepe. TOM WOODARD

Belt buckle and bola tie by Michael Kabotie, 1995. Bola tie is of three-layered silver overlay. LOVENA OHL GALLERY, SCOTTSDALE

designs are simple and elegant, and when he does use a stone it is an intrinsic part of the concept.

Michael Kabotie's father, Fred Kabotie, as well as being a well-known artist, was the design instructor for the veterans' classes. Michael learned to work silver by loitering around the guild workshop where Wally Sekayumptewa helped him. Later he worked alone while getting his college degree and achieving recognition as a painter himself. Michael's work in silver carries the dramatic impact of his painting. His layers of silver have the angular circular elements of his distinctive style, reminiscent of Awatovi murals but containing the clouds and rain, the bear and kachinas that are personal to him.

A totally new look in overlay is Richard Pawicki's version of the flute player. His use of fine line work and angular shapes becomes bits of movement across a bracelet or bola tie. His is an example of the continual flux of the Hopi jewelry craft. Each new smith brings his own view of the culture to add to the whole. The future holds exciting prospects in works of art from old craftsmen continuing to expand their horizons and newer smiths venturing into paths not yet explored.

7

HOPI SILVER HALLMARKS

➡ MUCH OF THE HOPI SILVER made now is stamped on the back with the smith's personal symbol. Hallmarks became widely used on Hopi silver during the veterans' classes in 1949. A few of the older smiths marked their silver in the 1930s. It may be noted that Mrs. Colton also urged them to do this in her letter of 1939. In 1938 the Indian Arts and Crafts Board authorized a stamp that said "U.S. Hopi" though it is doubtful that many items were marked with it. Silver produced under Hopi Silvercraft Guild auspices is marked with its insignia, the sun symbol, as well as with the individual smith's mark. Since ties with the guild were not constant, a man might buy silver himself, turn out a number of pieces and market them. At the same time he would be working for the guild. Thus in the same time period one might buy jewelry with both the guild mark and the smith's stamp, as well as pieces with only the smith's mark.

Workers for Hopicrafts formerly marked their silver with the firm's symbol only, with the exception of a few special pieces. Later, some of the smiths stamped their own initials on the Hopicrafts pieces regularly.

In the majority of instances, the marks used by the silversmiths are symbols of their clans. In theory, a clan is a group of people who trace their descent from a common ancestor. Among the Hopis, this line is carried through

Silver overlay jewelry by Richard Pawicki, 1997.

the women, so all the children belong to their mother's clan. Wiser heads than mine have tried to sort out Hopi clans and clan membership. In the succeeding list I have simply stated the clan that was given me by the smith himself or another Hopi. Many clans "go together." In these instances a symbol from any one of them is considered one's own clan symbol. Groups that are found in this list are: Sun, Sun's Forehead, and Eagle; Waterhouse (Patki) and Young Corn (Pikyas); Rabbit and Tobacco; Badger and Butterfly; Snake and Lizard; Bear, Strap, and Spider (Antelope also goes with this group); Snow and Fog; Kachina and Parrot.

In at least one known instance, the father's clan symbol was used. Other hallmarks were chosen for no obvious reason, since a smith could pick whatever mark he wished. In some instances, a hallmark may be reused—Vernon Mansfield is now using Willard Nuvayauoma's feather mark, but he doubles it.

Simply because a person is listed does not mean that he is, or was, a professional silversmith. I have tried to indicate, whenever possible, the extent of a smith's work. Even though a Hopi did no more work than that done in his veterans' classes, it is likely that pieces of his work are in the hands of the public. The class work was sold at the Indian Arts and Crafts Board Exhibit in Washington, D.C., the Hopi Craftsman Shows of the Museum of Northern Arizona, the Arizona State Fair in Phoenix, and at the Hopi Silvercraft Guild, when it was established. After the veterans' classes ended, new smiths learned their trade by working at the Hopi Guild.

The smiths are listed in approximately chronological order, based on available information. Following the list of silversmiths and their hallmarks, the marks are indexed by type to aid in their identification. Several shop marks have been included to aid in identifying Hopi jewelry. This does not imply shop endorsement or lack of it.

There are no hallmarks listed for many of the early smiths, since the

Silver jewelry showing hallmarks. LEFT TO RIGHT: *Ralph Tawangyaouma, Allen Pooyama, unknown.* KIM MESSIER

practice did not begin until the 1930s. For brevity, Hopi names are written in their traditional form, without hyphens or accents. Many of the smiths are known by several names, not including nicknames. The Hopis originally had no system of surnames, but were given new names to replace the old upon important occasions in their lives. Some of the names on the list are derived from this custom. Others have resulted from the children being given English names at school, which were used with their Indian names, and still others are the gradual development of a family name. Paul Andrew was the son of Andrew. He later used one of his Hopi names, Saufkie, as a last name, and now all his children use that as a last name. The Hopi today have one set of names for official use. The men may add the new name given by their godfathers at the Wuwuchim initiation. The index has attempted to list the various names by which a smith might be known today.

Many smiths have several villages listed under their residence. Among the Hopi a man customarily goes to live at his wife's home. Thus, normally, if he marries a woman from another village, he moves to his wife's village and becomes a resident there.

Several things are made apparent by the list of smiths. Among the men who took silversmithing under the G.I. Bill, less than half continued to work. However, this percentage may compare favorably with the results of any of the other veterans' training programs.

Sadder to note is the large number of silversmiths who have been killed. This may well reflect the high automobile accident rate among the Hopi as a whole. Another striking figure is the number of smiths who became blind or had to quit work because of poor eyesight. Again, the Hopi as a group are subject to eye maladies. However, John Adair in his discussion of Navajo silversmiths, calls eyestrain "the occupational disease of silversmithing." He also said that a smith could plan to do accurate work for only about twenty years before his eyes grew too weak to do silversmithing (Adair: 104). While most of the smiths working today have electric lights to see by, they also use acetylene torches a great deal, without any eye protection. Whether this actually contributes to deteriorating eyesight or not, the smiths feel it does. Whatever the causes, the list does show that a common reason for discontinuing silverwork is failing eyesight.

CHRONOLOGICAL LISTING
OF ARTISTS AND HALLMARKS

HALLMARK	SILVERSMITH	CLAN	VILLAGE	BEGAN SILVER WORK	WORKED SILVER UNTIL
No Mark	**Sikyatala**	**Mustard**	**Sichomovi**	ca. 1890	**d. after 1916**
No Mark	**Duwakuku**	**Mustard**	**Sichomovi**	pre-1900	**d. 1956**
	(Also: Tuwakuku) Born around 1865. Assume he began silverwork before 1900. Father of Hano potter, Garnet Pavatea.				
No Mark	**Andrew Humiquaptewa**	**Bluebird**	**Shungopavi**	pre-1900	**d. ca. 1962**
	A blacksmith who taught himself to make silver. Made brass objects before he worked silver. After the railroad reached Williams, Arizona (1882), took silver bracelets to the Havasupai and traded for buckskins.				
No Mark	**Tawahongniwa**	**Bear**	**Shungopavi**	pre-1900	**d. 1920**
No Mark	**Bert Fredericks**	**Bear**	**Oraibi**	ca. 1900	**d. 1960s**
	(Also: Sakwaitewa) Specialized in squash blossom necklaces and concha belts.				
No Mark	**Joshua Homiyesva**	**Sun**	**Shungopavi**	ca. 1900	**d. 1934**
	Son of Tawahongniwa. Started work at Carlisle. Demonstrated in San Diego in 1915.				
No Mark	**Silas Kewanwyma**	**Sun**	**Shungopavi**	ca. 1900	**d. 1932**
	(Also: Silas Yma) Son of Tawahongniwa. Entered silver in 1930 Hopi Craftsman Show.				
No Mark	**Lomawanu**	**Sun**	**Shungopavi**	ca. 1900	**d. ca. 1913**
	Son of Tawahonghiwa				
No Mark	**Washington Talayumptewa**	**Sun**	**Shungopavi**	ca. 1900	**d. 1963**
	(Also: Talaiumtewa) Son of Tawahongniwa. Continued silverworking until his death, but last entries in Hopi Craftsman Show were earrings of wood inlaid with turquoise.				
No Mark	**Tawanimptewa**	**Water Patki**	**Shungopavi**	ca. 1900	**ca. 1930 d. 1953**
	(Also: Tewaneptewa; Nickname: Sitakpu) Worked at Grand Canyon.				

HALLMARK	SILVERSMITH	CLAN	VILLAGE	BEGAN SILVER WORK	WORKED SILVER UNTIL
No Mark	**Tenakhongva** *Moved to Hotevilla at the Split.*	**Lizard**	**Oraibi-Hotevilla**	**ca. 1900**	**unknown**
No Mark	**Dan Kochongva** *(Also: Koitshongva, Kot-ka) Born in Oraibi but moved to Hotevilla at the Split. Half-brother of Sakhoioma. May be the Dan Kwiamawioma listed in Adair (1946) but no one seems to be familiar with the name.*	**Sun**	**Oraibi-Hotevilla**	**pre-1906**	**ca. 1940s d. 1972**
No Mark	**Sakhoioma** *Half-brother of Dan Kochongva. Moved to Hotevilla at the Split.*	**Sun Hotevilla**	**Oraibi-**	**pre-1906**	**ca. 1950**
No Mark	**Rutherford** *(Also: Tongeva, Tonagive, Duvama, Devayma, Durwyma) One of Tawahongniwa's five sons. Toured the United States demonstrating Hopi silversmithing, but made no more after he returned home.*	**Sun**	**Shungopavi**	**ca. 1930s**	**1936 d. 1962**
No Mark	**Sakewyumptewa** *(nickname: Sió) Called Sió, meaning "The Zuni," because he spent a lot of time at Zuni. I believe this is Adair's "Sakwiam."*	**Water Patki**	**Oraibi-Hotevilla**	**ca. 1907 -1912**	**d. after 1941**
No Mark	**Pierce Kewanwytewa** *(Also: Kewawytewa, Kwomáyowma) Maternal first cousin of Ralph Tawangyaouma. Married a Zia woman around 1934 and moved to Zia, but continued to make silver.*	**Corn**	**Oraibi**	**ca. 1906**	**d. 1960**
Thundercloud & H (Hopi)	**Ralph Tawangyaouma** *(Also: Tawagioma) Mark first used around 1930. Moved to Hotevilla at the Split. Did silversmithing in shops in Phoenix and Tucson until about 1964, when he moved back to Hotevilla.*	**Corn**	**Oraibi-Hotevilla**	**ca. 1906**	**d. 1973**
No Mark	**Roscoe Nuvasi** *(Also: Narvasi) Nephew of Sikyatala. Father of Perry Nuvasi. Still working in 1938.*	**unknown**	**Sichomovi**	**1915**	**1938**
Man's Head Scarf	**Earl Numkina** *Taught himself to make silver. Demonstrated silverwork at the Chicago World's Fair. Eyes failed in the 1940s.*	**Greasewood**	**Moenkopi**	**ca. 1920**	**1940s d. 1974**
Mark Not Definite	**Homer Vance** *(Also: Humiventewa) Born 1882. Worked at Grand Canyon for a year, as well as other stores.*	**Sun**	**Shipaulovi**	**ca. 1920**	**d. 1961**
No Mark	**Frank Nutaima** *Did excellent cast as well as stamped work. Eyes failed in the 1940s.*	**Rabbit**	**Moenkopi**	**pre-1920**	**1940s d. 1966**
No Mark	**Gene Nuvahoioma** *(Also: Jean; Nevahoioma, Nivowhioma; Pooyauma) Moved to Hotevilla at Split. Learned from Ralph, a first cousin of his wife, probably during 1920s. Was still working in 1930s. Son Allen Pooyama is a silversmith.*	**Coyote**	**Oraibi-Hotevilla**	**1920s**	**d. 1973**
Snow Cloud	**Paul Saufkie, Sr.** *(Also: Paul Andrew, Sifki) Son of Andrew Humiquaptewa. Learned from his father. Taught veterans' classes in silvermaking at Oraibi from 1948 to 1950. Made very little silver for fifteen years, but continued working till 1993.*	**Snow**	**Shungopavi**	**1920s**	

HALLMARK	SILVERSMITH	CLAN	VILLAGE	BEGAN SILVER WORK	WORKED SILVER UNTIL
Coyote Head & H	**Grant Jenkins**	Coyote	Oraibi-Moenkopi	pre-1924	d. ca. 1935
	First cousin of Harold Jenkins. Worked for jewelry stores in Phoenix and Flagstaff.				
Snake & H	**Morris Robinson**	Lizard	Oraibi-Bacavi	1924	d. 1987
	(Also: Talawytewa, Tealanwytewa) Mark used ca. 1931. Lived with Grant Jenkins in Phoenix and began to work silver then. Worked for many years as a silversmith. Retired in 1960s and returned to Bacavi. Did some cast work.				
No Mark	**Harold Jenkins**	Coyote	Oraibi-Moenkopi	ca. 1925	ca. 1939 d. 1949
No Mark	**Titus Lamson**	Saltbush	Hotevilla	ca. 1925	d. 1992
	Still doing silverwork in 1940s.				
No Mark	**Ben Setema**	Kachina	Oraibi	ca. 1925	unknown
	(Also: Setima)				
Snake & L.L.	**Lewis Lomay**	Masau	Oraibi	ca. 1930	d. 1996
	(Also: Lomayesva) Mark is from father's clan. Studied with Ambrose Roanhorse at Santa Fe Indian School. Worked at Frank Patania's silver shop for 13 years before going to another occupation. Continued his craftwork after retirement till his death. Did some cast work about 1949.				
No Mark	**Walter Muchka**	Badger	Oraibi	ca. 1930	killed 1938
	Worked with Lewis Lomay for Frank Patania while in Santa Fe. Killed at age twenty-five.				
No Mark	**Phillip Zi ayo ma, Jr.**	unknown	Mishongnovi	ca. 1930	d. 1960s
	(Also: Zeyouma) Made some silver when he had a store at the base of Mt. Elden in 1930, but later moved to Parker, Arizona.				
Masau	**Willie Coin**	Masau	Oraibi-Bacavi	1930	d. 1992
	(Also: Sitz wi isah) Used mark ca. 1948. Born in Oraibi, moved to Bacavi at marriage. Learned to make silver from his uncle, Earl Numkina, when they were acting in a San Gabriel Mission play in California.				
No Mark	**Arthur Masawytewa**	Eagle	Mishongnovi	1930s	killed 1952
	(Also: Arthur Hubbard) Was making silver in 1930s. Entered silver in the 1930 Hopi Craftsman Show.				
No Mark	**Harry A. Nasiwytewa**	Coyote	Oraibi	1930s	d. 1950
	Perhaps learned from Ralph Tawangyouma. Worked for stores in Phoenix. Was making silver in the 1930s.				
No Mark	**Ferris Setalla**	Millet	Walpi	1933	unknown
	Both he and his brother Robert learned from Randall Honwisioma in Phoenix.				
No Mark	**Robert Setalla**	Millet	Walpi	1933	killed 1940
	Born in Walpi, but married a woman of Moenkopi. Made a large amount of jewelry as a wholesale supplier to retail stores. His wife, Laura Payestewa, helped a little at times.				
Parrot	**Randall Honwisioma**	Parrot	Mishongnovi	pre-1933	1962
	(Also: Honwesima) Born 1906. Learned from Grant Jenkins at Graves Indian Store (later Skiles) in Phoenix. Worked for Vaughn's Indian Store in Williams, Arizona from 1937 to 1962. Almost blind in 1972.				

HALLMARK	SILVERSMITH	CLAN	VILLAGE	BEGAN SILVER WORK	WORKED SILVER UNTIL
Ear of Corn	Allen Pooyama	Corn	Hotevilla	ca. 1937	present
	(Also: Pooyaouma, Nuvahoyouma) Learned from his father, Gene Nuvahoyouma. Did commercial silverwork in Tucson for many years, but moved to Holbrook in 1970.				
No Mark	Eddie Scott, Sr.	Badger	Hotevilla	1937	killed 1951
	Learned from Allen Pooyama. Did commercial work in Flagstaff for Doc Williams' Saddlery Shop.				
Bear Claw	Marshall Jenkins	Bear	Oraibi-Bacavi	1939	d. 1982
	First used hallmark in 1967. Born Oraibi, moved to Bacavi at marriage. Learned from Chester Yellowhair at school in Alburquerque. Did little silverwork until 1960s when he moved from Navajo Ordnance Depot in Flagstaff back to Bacavi.				
1950-1955 DS Peyote Rain Bird	Preston Monongye	Grease-wood	Hotevilla	1939	d. 1987
	Used first mark shown from 1950 to 1955. Later used Peyote Rain Bird mark for some pieces and after 1965, used initials for his cast work. Worked in gold, as well as silver.				
Corn	Frieda Santiago	Masau	Kykotsmovi	late 1930s	ca. 1964
	Daughter of Jesse Posiomana. Learned techniques from Willie Coin. Married a Zuni man, Sylvester Santiago, and worked with him. They furnished Zuni style jewelry for various Indian craft stores. Quit because of impaired eyesight.				
Thunderhead	Sidney Sekakuku	Snow	Shungopavi	pre-1940	unknown
	Half-brother of Paul Saufkie and learned from him. Has not done silverwork for a long time.				
Tadpole	Harry Sakyesva	Corn	Hotevilla	ca. 1940s	d. 1971
	May have learned from Ralph Tawangyaoma and Allen Pooyama in Tucson. He was an excellent smith who continued to work though his health was very poor the last ten to fifteen years of his life.				
Rain Cloud	Victor Coochwytewa	Water Patki	Shungopavi	1940	present
	(Also: Victor Hugh) Originally worked with Paul Saufkie but also attended the veterans' classes. Has consistently made a quantity of jewelry for sale since then.				
Bear	Lawrence Saufkie	Bear	Shungopavi	1947	present
	Born 1935. Son of Paul Saufkie. Learned from his father when a teenager. After marriage began to do more silverwork.				
Tobacco Leaf	Everett Harris	Tobacco	Mishongnovi	1948 G.I. Bill	ca. 1951 killed 1968
	Has done very little since veterans' classes. Did very little after veteran's classes.				
Tobacco Flower	Calvin Hastings	Rabbit	Mishongnovi	1948 G.I. Bill	unknown
	Has not done silverwork for some time.				

HALLMARK	SILVERSMITH	CLAN	VILLAGE	BEGAN SILVER WORK	WORKED SILVER UNTIL
Butterfly	**Douglas Holmes** *Born Moenkopi, moved to Shungopavi at marriage.*	**Badger**	**Moenkopi- Shungopavi**	1948 G.I. Bill	1961
Lizard	**Neilson Honyaktewa** *Born Mishongnovi, moved to Shipaulovi at marriage. Has not done silverwork since veterans' classes.*	**Snake**	**Mishongnovi- Shipaulovi**	1948 G.I. Bill	ca. 1951
Nahsompi (Hair Whorl)	**Edgar Miller Hovalo** *Born Polacca, moved to Mishongnovi at marriage.*	**Kachina**	**Polacca- Mishongnovi**	1948 G.I. Bill	d. 1950s
Eagle	**Tom Humiyestiwa** *Did very little after veterans' classes.*	**Eagle**	**Mishongnovi**	1948 G.I. Bill	ca. 1951
Crescent Moon	**Valjean Joshevema, Sr.** *(Also: Lomaheftewa) Born Shungopavi, moved to Oraibi at marrige. Started silverwork again in the 1970's.*	**Sun**	**Shungopavi- Oraibi**	1948 G.I. Bill	present
Rattlesnake Head	**Richard Kagenvema** *(Pronounced: Kachin'-vema) Added fangs to the head of his silvermark about 1969.*	**Sun's Forehead**	**Shungopavi**	1948 G.I. Bill	d. 1982
Spider	**Herbert Komayouse** *(Also: Quimayousie)*	**Spider**	**Hotevilla**	1948 G.I. Bill	unknown
Star	**Harold Koruh** *Did very little after veterans' classes.*	**Sun**	**Mishongnovi**	1948 G.I. Bill	ca. 1951 d. 1992
Sun	**Samuel N. Laban**	**Sun's Forehead**	**Shipaulovi**	1948 G.I. Bill	d. 1955
War God	**Cortez Lomahukva** *(Also: Masayesva) Probably did very little silversmithing after veterans' classes.*	**Bear**	**Mishongnovi**	1948 G.I. Bill	ca. 1951
Antelope Rattle	**Charles T. Lomakima** *Worked about two and a half years during the silver classes.*	**Bear- Strap**	**Shungopavi**	1948 G.I. Bill	ca. 1951

HALLMARK	SILVERSMITH	CLAN	VILLAGE	BEGAN SILVER WORK	WORKED SILVER UNTIL
Squash	Kirkland Lomawaima	Squash	Shungopavi	1948 G.I. Bill	d. 1988
Bluebird	Starlie Lomayaktewa, Jr. _Had not done silversmithing for some time before 1972._	Bluebird	Mishongnovi	1948 G.I. Bill	unknown
Killdeer Track (Patsrokuku)	Clarence Lomayestewa _Has given tools to his brothers, Mark and McBride._	Snow	Shungopavi	1948 G.I. Bill	1964
Turtle	Eddie Nequatewa _Worked for about four years after veterans' classes._	Water Patki	Shungopavi	1948 G.I. Bill	d. 1985
Lightning	Dawson Numkina	Corn	Shipaulovi	1948 G.I. Bill	unknown
Rattlesnake Rattle	Walter Polelonema _Worked until his death._	Sun's Forehead	Shungopavi	1948 G.I. Bill	killed 1971
Sun's Forehead	Henry Polingyouma _Born Shungopavi, moved to Oraibi at marriage. Worked only during veterans' classes._	Sun's Forehead	Shungopavi- Oraibi	1948 G.I. Bill	ca. 1951
Crow Mother	Bert Puhuyestiwa _Had not done silversmithing for some time, before 1972._	Squash	Mishongnovi	1948 G.I. Bill	unknown
Crossed Arrows	Wallie Sekayumptewa _Quit in 1967 because of impaired eyesight. Was working a little in 1996. Eyesight had improved._	Reed	Hotevilla- Oraibi- Shungopavi	1948 G.I. Bill	
Cloud	Dean Siwingyumptewa _Brother of Lavern and Eldon. Had not done silverwork for some time, before 1972. Has given his tools to his brother Eldon._	Water- Patki	Mishongnovi	1948 G.I. Bill	unknown

HALLMARK	SILVERSMITH	CLAN	VILLAGE	BEGAN SILVER WORK	WORKED SILVER UNTIL
Tadpole	Lavern Siwingyumptewa	Water Patki	Mishongnovi	1948 G.I. Bill	
	Has given his tools to his brother Eldon. Had not done silverwork for some time before 1972.				
Mark Unknown	Nielson Suetopke	Parrot	Hotevilla	1948 G.I. Bill	unknown
Coyote	Dewan Sumatzkuku	Coyote	Hotevilla	1948 G.I. Bill	ca. 1951
	Didn't work after the veterans' classes.				
Pipe	Vernon Talas	Tobacco	Hano-Shungopavi	1948 G.I. Bil	d. 1985
	Born Hano, moved to Shungopavi at marriage. Had done blacksmithing before, so he made his own tools and some for others in the class.				
Bear Paw	Orville Talayumptewa	Bear	Bacavi	1948 G.I. Bil	unknown
Bear	Travis Yaiva	Bear	Oraibi	1948 G.I. Bil	not at present
Sun	Arthur Yowytewa	Sun	Oraibi-Bacavi	1948	
	Born Oraibi, moved to Bacavi at marriage. Quit in 1970 because of impaired eyesight. Eyesight improved and was working awhile in 1996.				
Tobacco Leaf	Edgar Coin	Rabbit	Oraibi	1948	unknown
	Did not attend veterans' classes.				
Rabbit Stick 1988	Ted Wadsworth	Bear	Shungopavi	1954	present
	(Also: Masungyouma) Brother-in-law of Victor Coochwytewa. Learned at the Guild.				
Star Priest	Leroy Kewanyama	Water Patki	Shungopavi	1955	1987 d. 1997
	Quit because of impaired eyesight. Learned at the Guild.				
Loloma	Charles Loloma	Badger	Hotevilla	1955	d. 1991
	Born 1921. Worked with Bob Winston, Fred Skaggs, and Morris Robinson. Made pottery before he worked silver.				

HALLMARK	SILVERSMITH	CLAN	VILLAGE	BEGAN SILVER WORK	WORKED SILVER UNTIL
 Snow Cloud	**Mark Lomayestewa** *Brother of Clarence and McBride. Learned at the Guild.*	**Snow**	**Shungopavi**	1955	**d. 1995**
 Lightning	**McBride Lomayestewa** *Brother of Mark and Clarence. Learned at the Guild.*	**Snow**	**Shungopavi**	1955	**d. 2002**
 Snow Cloud	**Bernard Dawakoya** *Learned first from his uncles, Washington Talayumpewa and Sidney Sekakuku and at the Guild Shop. Later worked for Hopicrafts when it opened in Phoenix and moved with them to the Kykotsmovi shop where he helped instruct their smiths. Now works for himself.*	**Snow**	**Shungopavi**	1956	**present**
 Spider	**Larson Onsae** *Was working in 1962. Learned at the Guild.*	**Bear-Strap**	**Shungopavi**	1957	**1960s**
 Star & Crescent Moon	**Billie Ray Hawee** *Born Shungopavi, moved to Hotevilla at marriage. Learned at the Guild.*	**Sun**	**Shungopavi-Hotevilla**	1959	**d. 1980**
 Orion 1967 Two Feathers 1970	**Vernon Mansfield** *He and Willard Nuvayaouma were first cousins. Willard gave him his tools and mark to use ca. 1967. Vernon had lost his mark, so started using the new one in 1970. Learned at the Guild.*	**Sun**	**Shungopavi**	1959	**present**
 Feather	**Willard Nuvayaouma** *Hadn't done any silverwork for some time previous to his death. Learned at the Guild.*	**Sun**	**Shungopavi**	1959	**killed 1969**
SEKAQUAPTEWA Sekaquaptewa	**Wayne & Emory Sekaquaptewa** *Learned from Harry Sakyesva. They owned and managed the Hopi Enterprises, later Hopicrafts shop, which crafted silverwork, as well as selling it wholesale and retail.*	**Eagle**	**Hotevilla**	1960	**Wayne d. 1979**
 Rabbit	**Eldon James** *Born Hotevilla, moved to Shungopavi at marriage. First worked at Hopicrafts when it opened in Phoenix, and moved with them to Kykotsmovi.*	**Rabbit**	**Hotevilla-Shungopavi**	1962	**d. 1979**
	Bradley Gashwazra *Born Oraibi, moved to Mishongnovi at marriage. Learned from Hopicrafts and worked for them.*	**Grease-wood**	**Oraibi-Mishongnovi**	1963	**present**

HALLMARK	SILVERSMITH	CLAN	VILLAGE	BEGAN SILVER WORK	WORKED SILVER UNTIL
B Lomadapki Joshweseoma	Robert Lomadapki-Joshweseoma	Fox (Pais)	Hotevilla	1964	present
	Studied at NAU with Tuck WIlliams and later with Jake Brookins.				
Snow Cloud 1965 / Snow Cloud 1972	Gracilda Saufkie	Fog	Shungopavi	1964	present
	Learned from her husband, Lawrence. Broke her first mark in 1971 and used new one in 1972.				
HONYAKTEWA	James Honyaktewa	Sun's Forehead	Shipaulovi	ca. 1965	present
	Learned at Santa Fe. Worked some years ago and started again in the 80's. Son of Neilson Honyaktewa.				
Snowflake 1965 / Cloud 1967	Patrick Lomawaima	Snow	Shungopavi	1965	present
	Son of Kirkland Lomawaima. Lost the Snowflake mark and started using the Cloud in 1967. Learned at the Guild.				
Snow Cloud	Manuel Poseyesva	Snow	Shungopavi-Sichomovi	1965	
	Born Shungopavi, moved to Sichomovi at marriage. Learned at Hopicrafts.				
Corn Plant 1975	Michael Sockyma	Corn	Hotevilla	1965	present
	Born Hotevilla, moved to Kykotsmovi upon marriage. Learned at Hopicrafts and worked for them. Later set up his shop at Kykotsmovi.				
Chief's Jug (Mong Wikoru)	Willie Archie Talaheftewa Dawungnufti	Corn	Shungopavi	1965	present
	Worked with his brother-in-law, Ted Wadsworth, and at the Guild.				
Father's Sun Symbol	Hubert Yowytewa	Reed	Bacavi	1965	d. 1991
	Learned from his father, Arthur Yowytewa, and at Hopicrafts. Used his initials with his father's symbol.				

HALLMARK	SILVERSMITH	CLAN	VILLAGE	BEGAN SILVER WORK	WORKED SILVER UNTIL
Spider	Norman Honie *Born Hano, moved to Shungopavi at marriage. Learned at the Guild.*	Spider	Hano-Shungopavi	1966	present
	Glenn Lucas *Born New Oraibi, moved to Mishongnovi at marriage. Learned at Hopicrafts and served as instructor.*	Sun	Kykotsmovi-Mishongnovi	ca. 1966	d. 1985
Snow Cloud 1990	Jason Takala *Worked with his maternal uncle, Bernard Dawahoya, at first. Also worked with Pierre Touraine.*	Snow	Shungopavi	1976	present
	Randall Sahmie *Learned at Santa Fe.*		Hano	1966–68	
	Bernard Dallasvuyama *Started with his uncle Charles Loloma, then worked on his own.*	Badger	Hotevilla–Albuquerque	1967	present
Friendship Mark	Phillip Honanie *Learned at Hopicrafts.*	Bear	Shungopavi	1967	present
1979	Michael Kabotie-Lomawywesa *Self-taught and helped by Wally Sekayumtewa. Little work till 1979.*	Snow	Shungopavi	1967	present
Sun's Forehead	Weaver Selina *Learned at Hopicrafts.*	Sun's Forehead	Shungopavi	1967	present
Rain Cloud	Emerson H. Quannie *Learned from Lawrence Saufkie.*	Water Patki	Kykotsmovi	1968	
Cloud	Eldon Siwingyumptewa Kalemsa, Sr. *Learned at the Guild.*	Snow	Mishongnovi	1968	d. 1996
1975	Nathan Fred, Jr. *Worked a short while in 1969, then quit until 1973 when he started using a silvermark.* *Learned at Hopicrafts.*	Greasewood	Bacavi	1969	present

HALLMARK	SILVERSMITH	CLAN	VILLAGE	BEGAN SILVER WORK	WORKED SILVER UNTIL
Rabbit Stick 1975	**Tony Kyasyousie** *Learned at Hopicrafts and worked there.*	**Grease-wood**	**Hotevilla**	1969	**d. 1993**
Ear of Corn	**Franklin Namingha** *Born Hotevilla, moved to Shungopavi at marriage. Learned at the Guild.*	**Corn**	**Hotevilla-Shungopavi**	1969	**present**
Antelope	**Arlo Nuvayaouma** *Moved to Phoenix in 1972 and not doing silverwork. Learned at the Guild.*	**Bear**	**Shungopavi**	1969	
R.M.V.S.S. 1987 GORE Used only on special orders	**Steven Sockyma** *Learned at Hopicrafts. Brother of Michael and Mitchell. New mark in 1987. In 1996 he was living in Glorieta, New Mexico.*	**Corn**	**Hotevilla**	1969	**present**
Spider both ca. 1977	**Gary and Elsie Yoyokie** *Learned at Hopicrafts. Graduated from high school in 1972 and has been working since.*	**Spider**	**Kykotsmovi**	1969	**present**
Bear paw	**Ricky Coochwytewa** *Learned from his father, Victor. His maternal uncle is Ted Wadsworth.*	**Bear**	**Shungopavi**	1970	
Corn Plant	**Kenneth Kuwanvayouma** *Learned at the Guild.*	**Corn**	**Shungopavi**	1970	**present**
Rabbit Stick 1977	**Daniel Phillips**	**Grease-wood**	**Oraibi**	1970	**present**
1975 1988 Feathers	**Jackson Seklestewa** *Learned at the Guild.*	**Eagle**	**Mishongnovi**	1970	**present**

HALLMARK	SILVERSMITH	CLAN	VILLAGE	BEGAN SILVER WORK	WORKED SILVER UNTIL
Corn Ear 1974	**Raymond Sequaptewa** *Learned at the Guild. Used initials when he first worked.*	**Corn**	**Hotevilla**	1970	present
Star	**Dalton Taylor** *Used the moon of Billie Rae Hawee's mark for a few pieces in 1973. Learned at the Guild.*	**Sun**	**Shungopavi**	1970	present
	Earl Yowytewa *Learned from father, Arthur Yowytewa.*	**Reed**	**Bacavi- Kykotsmovi**	1970	present
Pipe	**Joe Coochyumptewa** *Learned at the Guild.*	**Rabbit**	**Mishongnovi**	1971	
Antelope Track	**Ross Joseyesva** *Worked a little with Lawrence Saufkie and then went to Hopi Guild.*	**Strap**	**Shungopavi**	1971	present
	Jim Nutima *Learned at the Institute of American Indian Art, Santa Fe, and also worked with Preston Monongye.*	**Reed**	**Phoenix- Oraibi**	1971	
1974 Bear Paw ca. 1980	**Andrew Saufkie** *Son of Paul Saufkie. Learned from the Guild.*	**Bear**	**Shungopavi**	1971	
No Mark	**Roy Calnimptewa** *Learned from Eli Taylor in Oraibi.*	**Badger- Butterfly**	**Moenkopi- Oraibi-Phoenix**	1972	
Bear Paw 1975	**Marcus Coochwykvia** *Learned at Hopicrafts. Brother-in-law of Glenn Lucas.*	**Bear**	**Mishongnovi**	1972	present
Frog	**Aaron Honanie** *Learned at Hopicrafts. Uncle of Antone, brother of Ernest W. Honanie.*	**Fog**	**Shungopavi- Moenkopi**	1972	present
Hook for Bear Strap	**Jerry Honwytewa Whagado** *Learned at the Guild.*	**Spider**	**Shungopavi**	1970	present

HALLMARK	SILVERSMITH	CLAN	VILLAGE	BEGAN SILVER WORK	WORKED SILVER UNTIL
1972 1973 Rabbit Stick Rabbit Stick 1977	**Loren Phillips** *Learned at the Guild. Brother of Daniel. Three marks. Married to Fernanda Lomayestewa.*	Grease-wood	Oraibi	1972	d. 2001
Sun Symbol	**Roderick Phillips** *Cousin of Loren. Learned at the Guild.*	Sun	Oraibi	1972	present
1989 Bear Claws	**Riley Polyquaptewa**	Bear	Shungopavi	1972	
Antelope Track 1977 1988	**Sidney Sekakuku, Jr.** *Learned at the Guild.*	Strap	Shungopavi	1972	present
Initials	**Bob Sekakuku** *Self taught. Also watched uncle, Lawrence Saufkie.*	Sun's Forehead	Shipaulovi-Albuquerque-San Felipe	1972	
SICE *Sice*	**Howard Sice** *Self-taught. Hopi mother and Laguna father. Works with his Navajo wife, Patricia (Smith).*	Corn	Kykotsmovi	1972	present
Turtle 1975	**Mitchell Sockyma** *Born Hotevilla, moved to Kykotsmovi at marriage. Learned at Hopicrafts and worked for them. His mark varies in the relative position of the two initials in comparison with his brother Michael's identical initials.*	Corn	Hotevilla-Kykotsmovi	1972	present
Man	**Alvin Sosolde** *Learned from Bernard Dawahoya. Pima Indian married to Jason Takala's sister.*			1972	
Pipe	**Roy Tawahongva** *Also Tawahoingva. Learned at Hopicrafts.*	Rabbit	Hotevilla	1972	
	Virgil Thomas *Learned at Hopicrafts.*	Corn	Oraibi	1972	d. 1986

HALLMARK	SILVERSMITH	CLAN	VILLAGE	BEGAN SILVER WORK	WORKED SILVER UNTIL
Butterfly	**Verma Nequatewa**	**Badger**	**Hotevilla**	**1967**	**present**
	She and her sister Sherian Honhongva worked with their uncle, Charles Loloma. They first used "Sonwai" in 1972-73 for show pieces, and incorporated in 1989. In 1993 Sherian sold her shares and now uses a new mark.				
Snake Wand	**Lawrence Koyayesva** *Learned at the Guild.*	**Sun**	**Shungopavi**	**Started 1973 Came back 1988**	
Bear Paw	**Watson Honanie** *Learned from his brother, Phillip.*	**Bear**	**Shungopavi**	**1973**	**present**
Rattle	**Lauren Koinva** *Learned from Bernard Dawahoya.*	**Sun's Forehead**	**Shungopavi**	**1973**	**killed 1981**
Antelope Rattle	**Floyd Namingha Lomakuyvaya** *Learned from Kenneth Kuwanvayouma. Cousin of Raymie.*	**Strap**	**Shungopavi**	**1973**	
s P₃	**Starlie Polacca, III** *Studied in Santa Fe and then taught himself. His mark, a man, represents himself.*	**Tobacco**	**Parker, Arizona**	**1973**	**present**
LP ΠΠ Warrior Tracks / Sun Face	**Larry Polivema** *Learned from Hubert Yowytewa, ex brother-in-law.*	**Coyote**	**Oraibi-Bacavi**	**1973**	
1986	**Philbert Poseyesva** *Learned at Hopicrafts.*	**Bear**	**Mishongnovi-Oraibi**	**1973**	**present**
Tadpole 1976 / Tadpole 1986	**Loren Sakeva Qumawunu** *Was working for Bernard Dawahoya 1973. Now uses adult name received at initiation.*	**Corn**	**Shungopavi**	**1973**	

HALLMARK	SILVERSMITH	CLAN	VILLAGE	BEGAN SILVER WORK	WORKED SILVER UNTIL
	Courtney Amon Scott *Learned at Hopicrafts.*	Sun	Kykotsmovi	1973	present
	Elgene Sehongva *Learned at Hopicrafts. Mark first used in late 1973.*	Corn	Hotevilla	1973	
1980	**Phillip Sekaquaptewa** *Learned at Hopicrafts. Son of Wayne.*		Hotevilla	1973	d. 2002
Tadpole NHJR	**Norman Honie, Jr.** *Learned from his father, Norman.*	Fog	Shungopavi	1974	
AH Initials	**Anthony Honahnie** *An artist, he made designs for various smiths then decided to design for himself. Has the coyote stamp of Dewan Sumatskuku but doesn't use it.*	Coyote	Moenkopi-Phoenix	1974	
Bear Paw	**Winfield Humeyestewa** *Learned at Hopicrafts. Brother of Jay and Bryan.*	Bear	Mishongnovi	1974	d. 1992
Hopping Frog	**Wilmer Kavena** *Introduced to silverwork and lapidary in 1939 at Keams Canyon shop class, teacher Corbert Grant.*	Rabbit	Sichomovi	1974	
Sun's Forehead	**Elliot Koinva** *Learning from Hopi Guild. Brother of Lauren. Both are grandsons of Paul Saufkie.*	Sun's Forehead	Shungopavi	1974	present
Parrot New Mark 1987	**Duane Maktima** *Studied with Victor Beck and then Jake Brookins. His mother is Laguna Indian and his father is from Hotevilla. He was living in Glorieta, New Mexico, in 1977.*	Parrot		1974	present

HALLMARK	SILVERSMITH	CLAN	VILLAGE	BEGAN SILVER WORK	WORKED SILVER UNTIL
Antelope	**Verden Mansfield** *Learned from his father, Vernon Mansfield.*	**Strap**	**Shungopavi**	1974	**present**
No Mark	**Phil Navasya** *Studied at CSU, Fresno, California with Ed Lund.*	**Corn**	**Oraibi**	1974	**present**
	Sharold Nutumya *Learned at Hopicrafts.*	**Parrot**	**Oraibi-Mishongnovi**	1974	
Medicine Bowl (Nakwichakafta) Chief's Jug (Mong Wikoru)	**Steven Pooyouma Kuyvaya** *Son of Allen Pooyama (Young Corn). First worked at Hopicrafts. Used initials at first. Medicine Bowl used ca. 1977.*		**Hotevilla**	1974	
	Bobby Tewa *His mother is San Juan and his father is from Bacavi. Learned as an apprentice in San Juan jewelry program.*	**Winter**	**San Juan**	1974	
Bear Fangs	**Ronald Youvella** *Learned at the Guild.*	**Bear**	**Mishongnovi**	1974	
	Gilbert Andress Tyma *Learned at Hopicrafts.*	**Sun's Forehead**	**Shungopavi**	1975	
Fox Ears & Initials, Fox	**Art Batala** *Learned at Hopicrafts (Glenn Lucas).*	**Masau**	**Mishongnovi**	1975	**present**
Snow Cloud 1990s	**Bueford Dawahoya** *Also spelled Beauford and Beuford. Worked first with his brother, Bernard.*	**Snow**	**Shungopavi**	1960's	**present**
	Alfonso Gashwazra *Learned at Hopicrafts. Brother of Bradley and uncle of Loren Phillips.*	**Grease-wood**	**Oraibi**	1975	

HALLMARK	SILVERSMITH	CLAN	VILLAGE	BEGAN SILVER WORK	WORKED SILVER UNTIL
	Emery Holmes	**Badger**	**Moenkopi**	**1975**	
	Learned at Hopicrafts (Glenn Lucas). Brother of Douglas.				
Strong Rain	**Manuel Hoyungwa**	**Grease-wood**	**Hotevilla**	**1975**	**present**
	Worked with his maternal uncle, Preston Monongye, and also studied at the Institute of American Indian Art, Santa Fe.				
	Bryan Humeyestewa	**Bear**	**Mishongnovi**	**1975**	
	Learned at Hopicrafts. Brother of Jay and Winfield.				
No Mark	**Helen Joshevema**	**Corn**	**Oraibi**	**1975**	**unknown**
	Learned by watching her father, Valjean Joshevema.				
	Raymond Kyasyousie	**Grease-wood**	**Hotevilla**	**1975**	
	Learned at Hopicrafts (Glenn Lucas). Brother of Tony.				
Rabbit Track	**Philbert Polingyouma**	**Rabbit**	**Oraibi**	**1975**	**d. 1982**
	Learned at Hopicrafts. Son of Henry Polingyouma.				
Young Corn	**Larry (Lawrence) Pooyouma**		**Hotevilla**	**1975**	**d. 1991**
	Son of Allen Pooyama (Young Corn). First worked at Hopicrafts.				
Bear Paw	**Alde Qumyintewa**	**Bear**	**Shungopavi**	**1975**	
	Learned at the Guild.				
Antelope Horn	**Myron Sekakuku**	**Strap**	**Shungopavi-Shipaulovi**	**1975**	
	Learned at the Institute of American Indian Art, Santa Fe. Mark probably used in 1977. Brother of Sydney, Jr.				
	Doran Sehongva Puhudawa	**Bear**	**Shipaulovi**	**1975**	
	Learned at Hopicrafts.				

HALLMARK	SILVERSMITH	CLAN	VILLAGE	BEGAN SILVER WORK	WORKED SILVER UNTIL
No Mark	**Henry Shelton**	Tobacco	**Moenkopi-Hotevilla**	**1975**	
	Learned at the Santa Fe Indian School from a Navajo smith, Jack Smith, in 1949. Did some silverwork in 1975 but mostly carves kachinas.				
Frog	**Terry Wadsworth**	Corn	**Shungopavi**	1975	
	Learned from his father, Ted Wadsworth.				
HT	**Hubert Taylor**	Grease-wood	**Polacca**	1975–78	
	Learned by watching other smiths. Father is Dalton Taylor.				
Corn Plant	**William Setalla**	Corn	**Oraibi**	Pre-1976	**present**
	Married to a Pima woman at Sacaton. Son of Robert Setalla.				
1984 Sun Face 1984 / 1984 Sun Face 1995	**Charles Supplee**	Sun	**Kykotsmovi**	1975	**present**
	Studied with Pierre Touraine after he had learned the rudiments himself. Father is non-Indian of French descent.				
Tobacco Leaf	**John Coochyumptewa (JLC)**	Rabbit (Tobacco)	**Mishongnovi**	1976	
	Learned at the Guild. Uncle of Joe.				
1981 / C. DAY / Cloud 1982	**Chalmers Day**	Corn	**Kykotsmovi-Albuquerque**	1976	
	Started in Manpower Class, Phoenix, taught by Preston Monongye, then worked for him. Stepfather is Paul Day, Parrot Clan, Laguna Pueblo.				
Bear Claws	**Jay Humeyestewa**	Bear	**Mishongnovi**	1976	
	Brother of WInfield and Bryan.				

HALLMARK	SILVERSMITH	CLAN	VILLAGE	BEGAN SILVER WORK	WORKED SILVER UNTIL
 War God	**Cedric (Navenma) Kuwaninvaya** *Now uses adult name received at initiation. Learned at the Guild.*	Sun's Forehead	**Shipaulovi**	1976	
 Lightning & Spider LOMAHEFTEWA 	**Marvin Lomaheftewa** *Worked first with Lee Carroll at NAU. Valjean Joshevema was his uncle.*	Spider	**Hotevilla-Shungopavi**	1976	**d. 1986**
 FLute Chief Stick	**Marcus Lomayestewa** *Son of McBride Lomayestewa. Learned at the Guild.*	Bear	**Shungopavi**	1976	
 Corn	**Delbert Nevayaktewa** *Learned at the Guild.*	Corn	**Mishongnovi**	1976	
 Spider	**Grant Pawiki** *Learned at the Guild.*	Spider	**Hotevilla**	1976	
 Feather	**Jacob Poleviyouma, Jr. (JPJR)** *Learned at the Guild.*	Sun	**Shungopavi-Hotevilla**	1976	**d. 1986**
 Bluebird Track	**Harvey Quanimptewa, Jr.** *Learned at the Guild.*	Bluebird-Spider	**Mishongnovi**	1976	**d. 1993**
	Eddie Scott, Jr. *Son of Eddie Scott, Sr., brother of Courtney.*	Sun	**Kykotsmovi**	1976	**present**

HALLMARK	SILVERSMITH	CLAN	VILLAGE	BEGAN SILVER WORK	WORKED SILVER UNTIL
Waterbug / New Mark 1990	**Roy Talahaftewa** *Learned from brother, Willie.*	Corn	Shungopavi	1976	present
Sun / 1989	**Milson Taylor** *Learned at the Guild.*	Sun	Shungopavi	1976	present
Snow Cloud	**Pat Tewawina** *Learned at the Guild.*	Snow	Shungopavi	1976	present
One-Horn (Society)	**Steward Tewawina Dacawyma** *Nephew of Bernard Dawahoya and brother of Pat. Learned at the Guild.*	Snow	Shungopavi	1976	present
RAMONA	**Ramona Poleyma** *Sister of Charles Loloma, aunt of Verma and Sherian.*	Badger	Hotevilla	ca. 1977	1978
MJ	**Murray Jackson** *Married to Fermina Nutumya. Learned at Hopicrafts.*	Walapai Tribe	Oraibi	1977	
DALANGYAWMA 1989 / R	**Ramon (Albert, Jr.) Dalangyawma** *Learned at Hopicrafts. Navajo mother.*		Hotevilla	1978	present
HN	**Stephen Hyson Naseyoma** *Learned at Hopicrafts (Glenn Lucas).*	Grease-wood	Hotevilla-Shungopavi	1978	
Road Runner	**Edward Lomahongva (Phillips)** *Learned at Hopicrafts.*	Grease-wood	Oraibi	1979	

HALLMARK	SILVERSMITH	CLAN	VILLAGE	BEGAN SILVER WORK	WORKED SILVER UNTIL
(hallmark image) Carried in Beauty	**Preston Duwyenie (Loma-i-quil-via)** *Attended IAIA and also Colorado State Univ., Nelda Getty, instructor.*	Reed	Hotevilla	1980	present
KOOTSWATEWA 1980	**Loren Kootswatewa** *Learned at Hopicrafts from Sekaquaptewa brothers.*	Sand	Hotevilla	1960	
(antelope images) Talasventiwa Antelope	**Arthur Allen Lomayestewa** *Son of Mark Lomayestewa. Talasventewa is his new name but he only uses it on jewelry.*	Strap	Shungopavi	1980	present
(sun image) Sun	**Fernanda Lomayestewa** *Daughter of Clarence. Learned at the Guild.*	Sun	Shungopavi	1980	
(hallmark images) NR 1988 Rattlesnake Rattle	**Raymie Namingha** *Learned at Hopicrafts. He uses the mark of his maternal uncle, Walter Polelonema.*	Sun's Forehead	Shungopavi	1978	
(snowflake images) 1990s Snowflake, J Initials, Snowflake	**Jesse Josytewa** *Learned from Bernard Dawahoya.*	Snow	Shungopavi	1982	present
(spider image) Little Spider	**Bennett Kagenvema** *Learned from father, Richard, and the Guild.*	Strap	Shungopavi	1982	present
(antelope head image) Antelope Head	**Dwayne Lomayestewa** *Learned at the Guild. Son of Mark.*	Strap	Shungopavi	1982	
(T L d image)	**Trinidad "Trini" Lucas** *Learned from her father, Glenn Lucas. Married to Tim Mowa.*	Bear	Mishongnovi	1982	present

HALLMARK	SILVERSMITH	CLAN	VILLAGE	BEGAN SILVER WORK	WORKED SILVER UNTIL
 1990s	Marvin Lucas Naquahyeoma *Learned from his father, Glenn Lucas. Wife is Effie Tawahongva.*	Bear	Mishongnovi	1982	present
 Lakon Corn	Ronald Wadsworth *Learned at the Guild and from father Ted Wadsworth.*	Corn	Shungopavi	1982	present
	Cleve Honyaktewa *Learned from Phil Sekaquaptewa, Emery Holmes, Honani Crafts. Younger brother of James.*	Sun's Forehead	Shipaulovi	1983	d. 1996
 Bear Paw	Willis Humeyestewa *Learned at the Guild. Brother of Bryan, Larry, Jay, and Winfield.*	Bear	Mishongnovi	1983	
 Shooting Star	Lendrick Lomayestewa *Learned at the Guild. Son of Clarence.*	Sun	Shungopavi	1983	
 Star & Moon	Stetson Lomayestewa *Son of Clarence. Billie Ray's hallmark always had the moon underneath the star.*	Sun	Shungopavi	1983	
 1995 Star	Terrance Lomayestewa *Learned at the Guild. Son of Clarence.*	Sun	Shungopavi	1983	present
 Antelope	Benjamin Mansfield *Learned at the Guild. Son of Vernon Mansfield.*	Strap	Shungopavi	1983	
 Sun, Star, & Moon	Augustine Mowa, Jr. *Learned at the Guild.*	Sun	Shungopavi	1983	
 Quarter Sun	Clifton Mowa *Learned at the Guild. Brother of Augustine, Jr.*	Sun	Shungopavi	1983	

HALLMARK	SILVERSMITH	CLAN	VILLAGE	BEGAN SILVER WORK	WORKED SILVER UNTIL
Spider *Poleviyuma*	**Harrington Poleviyuma** *Learned at the Guild. Son of Jacob, Jr. Started using name in early 1990s.*	**Strap**	Shungopavi	1983	present
Flute Rattle	**James Selina** *Learned at the Guild. Son of Weaver Selina's brother, Vincent.*	**Snow**	Shungopavi	1983	
Rabbit	**Mark Tawahongva** *Learned at the Guild. Son of Berra.*	**Rabbit**	Hotevilla	1983	
Sun's Forehead	**Shannon Lamson** *Learned at the Guild. He is now using brother's mark (1989).*	**Sun's Forehead**	Shungopavi	1984	present
Half Sun & Initial	**David Mowa** *Learned at the Guild. Brother of Augustine, Jr.*	**Sun**	Shungopavi	1984	
Sun's Mouth	**Tim Mowa** *Learned at the Guild. Husband of Trini Lucas, brother of Augustine, Jr.*	**Sun**	Shungopavi	1984	present
Half Sun & Eagle	**Wilson Mowa** *Learned at the Guild. Brother of Augustine, Jr.*	**Sun**	Shungopavi		
Sun's Forehead & Corn Plant	**Leonard Shupla, Jr.** *Learned at the Guild.*	**Sun's Forehead**	Shungopavi	1984	
Masau-u	**Berra Tawahongva** *Learned at the Guild.*	**Coyote**	Mishongnovi	1984	
CW	**Cheryl Wadsworth Soohafyah** *Works with her husband, Eddison Wadsworth Soohafyah. SIster of Berra Tawahongva.*	**Coyote**	Mishongnovi	1986	present

HALLMARK	SILVERSMITH	CLAN	VILLAGE	BEGAN SILVER WORK	WORKED SILVER UNTIL
Lakota Rain Mark	Eddison Wadsworth Soohafyah *Learned at the Guild and from father, Ted Wadsworth.*	Corn	Shungopavi	1984	present
Eagle	Courtney Mahkee	Eagle	Mishongnovi	c. 1985	
Initials with Snake	Peggy Lomay *Learned from her father, Lewis Lomay.*		Santa Fe	1985	present
Sun's Forehead	Delmar Lamson *Learned at the Guild.*	Sun's Forehead	Shungopavi	1985	d. 1988
Bald Eagle	Roger Selina *Learned at the Guild. Brother of James.*	Snow	Shungopavi	1985	
Initails with Snake 1989 (new mark)	Irvin Lomay *Learned from his father, Lewis Lomay.*		Santa Fe	1986	present
Star Priest	Harold Lomayaktewa *Learned at the Guild. His uncle, Leroy Kewanwytewa, used this mark until he quit silversmithing because of eye trouble.*	Water Patki	Shungopavi	1986	present
Sun's Face	Moody Lomayaktewa *Learned at the Guild. Nephew of Walter Polelonema.*	Sun's Forehead	Shungopavi	1986	
Eagle Beak	Tyler Polelonema *Learned at the Guild. Brother of Walter.*	Sun's Forehead	Shungopavi	1986	

HALLMARK	SILVERSMITH	CLAN	VILLAGE	BEGAN SILVER WORK	WORKED SILVER UNTIL
Parrot	**Jaylene Takala** *Learned from father, Jason. Started when she was 8 years old.*	**Parrot**	**Oraibi**	**1986**	
Bear Paw	**Gerald Honwytewa** *Learned at the Guild. Son of Jerry Honwytewa Whagado, nephew of Pascal Nuvamsa.*	**Bear**	**Shungopavi**	**1987**	
Antelope Rattle	**Larry Humeyestewa** *Learned at the Guild. Brother of Bryan, Jay, Winfield, Willis.*	**Bear**	**Mishongnovi**	**1987**	
Kuwanhongva Flute Player	**Pascal Nuvamsa Kuwanhongva** *Learned at the Guild. McBride Lomayestewa's son.*	**Bear**	**Shungopavi**	**1987**	**present**
Initials with Snake	**James Rawn Lomay** *Learned from his grandfather. Son of Irvin.*		**Santa Fe**	**1987**	
DL 1994	**Dawn Lucas** *Learned from her uncle, Marcus Coochwykvia. Daughter of Glenn Lucas. Married to Fernando Batala.*	**Bear**	**Mishongnovi**	**1987**	**present**
HL HNL 1991	**Helena Lucas Namingha** *Learned from her husband, Raymie Namingha. Daughter of Glenn Lucas.*	**Bear**	**Mishongnovi**	**1987**	**present**
EH Sun's Forehead	**Edward Nequatewa** *Learned at the Guild. Eddie (Edmund, Jr.) Nequatewa's son.*	**Sun's Forehead**	**Shungopavi**	**1987**	**d. 1991**
R P Spider	**Richard Pawicki** *Learned at the Guild. Brother of Grant.*	**Spider**	**Hotevilla**	**1987**	**present**

HALLMARK	SILVERSMITH	CLAN	VILLAGE	BEGAN SILVER WORK	WORKED SILVER UNTIL
Spider	**Marvin Sekayesva** _Learned at the Guild._	**Bluebird**	**Hotevilla**	**1987**	
Snow Flake / Waterbird, & Flute Flower	**Michael Selina** _Brother of James. Learned at the Guild._	**Snow**	**Shungopavi**	**1987**	**d. 1997**
	Philbert Selina _Learned at the Guild. Brother of James._	**Snow**	**Shungopavi**	**1987**	**present**
Snow Balls / 1995	**Vinton Selina** _Brother of James._	**Snow**	**Shungopavi**	**1987**	**present**
Rain-Wave	**Perry Fred** _Learned at the Guild. Son of Nathan Fred, Jr. When he makes the piece, he uses his initials. When he and Petra Lamson both work on a piece they use the combined initials._	**Fog**	**Shungopavi**	**1988**	**d. 1999**
	Leroy Honyaktewa _Learned from Glenn Lucas. Cousin of Jackson Seklestewa._	**Eagle**	**Mishongnovi**	**1988**	**present**
Eagle's Claw	**Robert Honyaktewa** _Learned at the Guild. Brother of Leroy and son of Neilson._	**Eagle**	**Mishongnovi**	**1988**	
Snowman	**Cyrus Josytewa, Jr.**	**Snow**	**Shungopavi**	**1993**	
Snowflake	**Guy Josytewa** _Learned at the Guild. Brother of Jesse._	**Snow**	**Shungopavi**	**1988**	

HALLMARK	SILVERSMITH	CLAN	VILLAGE	BEGAN SILVER WORK	WORKED SILVER UNTIL
Snowflake & Name	Joe Josytewa *Learned from brothers Jesse and Louie.*	Snow	Shungopavi	1988	
Tree Stump	Duwayne Kopelva *Learned at the Guild. His name means tree stump.*	Coyote	Moenkopi	1988	
Antelope Head	Danny Kuwanvayouma *Learned at the Guild.*	Strap	Shungopavi	1988	
Bear Paw	Malcorbin Lomakema *Learned at the Guild. Father was Millard Lomakema. Grandson of Paul Saufkie, Sr.*	Bear	Shungopavi	1988	d. 1994
Sun's Forehead	Jack Nequatewa *Learned at Guild. Brother of Edward.*	Sun's Forehead	Shungopavi	1988	present
	Lambert Poseyesva *Learned from brother Philbert.*	Bear	Mishongnovi	1988	present
Rain & Lightning	Ruben Saufkie *Learned from the Guild. Paul, Jr.'s son.*	Water-Patki	Shungopavi	1988	
Initials	Darren Seweyestewa *Learned from Mitchell Sockyma. Uncle is Robert Lomadapki.*	Coyote	Hotevilla	1988	
	Gary Shupla *Learned at the Guild.*	Sun's Forehead	Shungopavi	1988	
Rainbow	Maynard Talaheftewa *Learned at the Guild. Brother of Roy and Willie.*	Corn	Shungopavi	1988	present

HALLMARK	SILVERSMITH	CLAN	VILLAGE	BEGAN SILVER WORK	WORKED SILVER UNTIL
	Tony (Anthony) Burton *Honani Crafts trainee. Cousin of Phil Navasya.*	**Corn**	**Oraibi**	**1989**	**d. 1993**
1995 Cloud & Pahos	**Harlan Joseph** *Learned at Honani Crafts.*	**Snow**	**Shungopavi**	**1989**	
BK Spider	**Brian Kagenvema** *Nephew of Bennett Kagenvema.*	**Strap**	**Shungopavi**	**1989**	**present**
Sun's Forehead & Rain Cloud	**Eldon Kalemsa, Jr.** *Learned from father Eldon Kalemsa, Sr. Mark first used in 1989.*	**Sun's Forehead**	**Shungopavi**	**1982**	**present**
Yaya's Rattle LK 1995 MLK with wife	**Lucion Koinva** *Lost rattle mark so started using initials in 1995. Learned at the Guild and from Sidney Sekakuku, Jr. Married to Melinda Lucas.*	**Sun's Forehead**	**Shungopavi**	**1989**	**present**
LM	**Loren Maha** *Learned from Norman Honie, Sr.*	**Spider**	**Tewa**	**1989**	**present**
	Effie Tawahongva Naquahyeoma *Learned from husband Marvin Lucas and brother Berra Tawahongva.*	**Coyote**	**Mishongnovi**	**1989**	
Bear Claw	**Rosella Nutumya** *Guild trainee.*	**Bear**	**Mishongnovi**	**1989**	
GP	**George Phillips** *Learned at the Guild. Brother of Loren Phillips.*	**Saltbush**	**Oraibi**	**1989**	

HALLMARK	SILVERSMITH	CLAN	VILLAGE	BEGAN SILVER WORK	WORKED SILVER UNTIL
Initials	Dorothy Poleyma Kyasyousie *Learned from husband, Raymond. Daughter of Ramona Poleyma.*	Badger	Hotevilla	1989	
Puhuhefvaya Snow Cloud	Fernando Puhuhefvaya *Learned from Guild. Brother of Pat Tewawina and Steward Dacawyma.*	Snow	Shungopavi	1989	
ESS III	Eddie Stirling Scott, III *Learned from his father, Eddie Scott II.*	Tobacco	Kykotsmovi	1989	
Initials	Merle Sehongva *Learned from Doran Sehongva.*	Bear	Shipaulovi	1989	
Flute Player & Name	Don Supplee *Learned from brother, Charles Supplee, and Roy Talaheftewa.*	Sun	Kykotsmovi	1989	present
Snow Flake	Jayme Takala (Nuva-lawu) *Learning from father, Jason. Entered Juvenile Show at Heard Museum in 1989. Name means snowing.*	Parrot	Oraibi	1989	
Frog	Charlotte Joshua Andrews *Learned from Guild; granddaughter of Joshua.*	Water Patki	Shungopavi	1990	
Dewakuku	Reginald Dewakuku *Learned from Phillip Sekaquaptewa.*	Sun's Forehead	Shipaulovi	1990	
Left Eagle Wing	Marian Gashwazra *Learned at the Guild. Father is Bradley Gashwazra. Deceased husband Roy Wing (Navajo). Left wing smaller than sister Elsie Gashwazra's.*	Eagle	Mishongnovi	1990	
Sun's Forehead	Melson Harris *Learned at the Guild. Grandson of Starlie Lomayaktewa, Sr.*	Sun's Forehead	Shipaulovi	1990	

HALLMARK	SILVERSMITH	CLAN	VILLAGE	BEGAN SILVER WORK	WORKED SILVER UNTIL
Sun's Forehead	**Michael Harris** *Learned at the Guild. Brother of Melson.*	**Sun's Forehead**	**Shipaulovi**	1990	
Yaya's Rattle	**Ernest Honyaktewa** *Learned from brother Robert Honyaktewa.*	**Eagle**	**Mishongnovi**	1990	
Sun's Forehead & Arrow	**Duane Koinva** *Father is Eldridge Koinva.*	**Sun's Forehead**	**Shungopavi-Shipaulovi**	1990	
Sun's Forehead & Feather	**Leon Lomakema** *Learned from Clifton Mowa. Cousin of Palmer.*	**Sun's Forehead**	**Shungopavi**	1990	
Frog	**Wilmer Saufkie Lomayouma** *Learned from father and mother, Lawrence and Gracilda Saufkie. Little work until 1993.*	**Fog**	**Shungopavi**	1990	
Initials	**Lucy Lucas** *Learned from father, Glenn Lucas. Married to Leroy Honyaktewa.*	**Bear**	**Mishongnovi**	1990	
Sun	**Greg Naseyouma**	**Sun**	**Oraibi-Moenkopi**	1990	
Bird Track	**Joel Nasonhoya** *Learned at the Guild.*	**Road-runner**	**Sichomovi**	1990	
Bear Paw	**Elmer Setalla Jr.** *Self taught. Worked with Watson Honanie.*	**Bear**	**Shungopavi Polacca**	1990	
EVA Corn Plant & Name	**Evanette Sockyma** *Learned from her father, Michael Sockyma, Sr.*	**Bear**	**Kykotsmovi**	1990	
J.R. Corn Plant	**Michael C. Sockyma, Jr.** *Learned from father, Michael Sockyma, Sr.*	**Bear**	**Kykotsmovi**	1990	

HALLMARK	SILVERSMITH	CLAN	VILLAGE	BEGAN SILVER WORK	WORKED SILVER UNTIL
KTK (Kevin Takala)	Kevin Takala *Learned from his brother Jason Takala.*	Snow	Shungopavi	1990	
Kopituvuh Breath of the Sun	Alvin Taylor *Learned from nephew Milson Taylor and Clifton Mowa.*	Sun	Shungopavi-Kykotsmovi	1990	
Lightning & Tadpoles	Meredith Van Winkle *Learned at the Guild. Charlotte Andrew's daughter.*	Water Patki	Shungopavi	1990	
E A	Everett Adams *Self-taught.*	Strap Spider-Bear	Shungopavi-Walpi	1991	present
Crow Mother	Howard Dennis *Learned at the Guild; nephew of Bert Puhuyestiwa.*	Squash	Mishongnovi	1991	
Initials	Caroline Fred (Mansfield) *Benjamin Mansfield's wife, daughter of Nathan Fred, Jr.; learned from them.*	Fog	Shungopavi	1991	
Initials	Julian Fred *Worked with his brother, Perry. Son of Nathan Fred, Jr.*	Fog	Shungopavi	1991	
Right Eagle Wing	Elsie Gashwazra *Father is Bradley Gashwazra. Right wing larger than sister Marian Gashwazra's.*	Eagle	Mishongnovi	1991	
MG G	Michael Gashwazra *Son of Bradley Gashwazra.*	Eagle	Mishongnovi	1991	
00 o o Rabbit Track	Fermin Hawee *Learned at the Guild. Uses the tools of his father, Billy Rae Hawee.*	Rabbit	Hotevilla	1991	
CH	Clement Honie *Started guild classes, but continued training with his father Norman Honie.*	Fog	Shungopavi	1991	present

HALLMARK	SILVERSMITH	CLAN	VILLAGE	BEGAN SILVER WORK	WORKED SILVER UNTIL
Water Loon	**John Honie** *Guild class. Son of Norman Honie.*	**Fog**	**Shungopavi**	1972	**present**
HONVENTEWA	**Alfred Honventewa** *Terrance and Carol Talaswaima's son. Learned from Phil Sekaquaptewa.*		**Mishongnovi**	1991	
RH	**Ryan Honyaktewa** *Neilson Honyaktewa Jr.'s son*	**Fog**	**Kykotsmovi**	1991	
MLK Initials with husband	**Melinda Lucas Koinva** *Learned from Lucas family. Father was Glenn Lucas.*	**Bear**	**Mishongnovi**	1991	**present**
Quarter Sun's Forehead	**Petra Lamson** *Uses her brother's former sun mark if she cuts the piece. If she just helps with finishing she and Perry Fred use the combined initials.*	**Sun's Forehead**	**Shungopavi**	1991	
Cloud & Corn	**Charleston Lewis** *Learned at the Guild. Cousin of Ryan Kuyvaya.*	**Fog**	**Shungopavi**	1991	**present**
Snake	**Raymond Lomaheitewa** *Learned at the Guild.*	**Snake**	**Mishongnovi**	1991	**present**
Bear Paw	**Ila Lomawaima** *Learned at the Guild. Daughter of Patrick Lomawaima.*	**Bear**	**Shungopavi**	1991	
NL	**Nadine Lalo Lomawunu** *Learned from her father Eldon Kalemsa, Sr. Wife of William Lalo Lomawunu.*	**Sun's Forehead**	**Shungopavi**	1991	
WL Cloud	**William Lalo Lomawunu** *Taught himself by watching Eldon Kalemsa, Sr.*	**Coyote**	**Sichomovi**	1991	**unknown**
Spider & Web	**Vern Mansfield** *Learned at the Guild. Son of Vernon Mansfield.*	**Strap**	**Shungopavi**	1991	**present**

HALLMARK	SILVERSMITH	CLAN	VILLAGE	BEGAN SILVER WORK	WORKED SILVER UNTIL
Bear Paw	**Darren Masawytewa** *Learned at the Guild. Grandson of Arthur Masawtewa. Nickname "Wiki."*	**Bear**	**Mishongnovi**	1991	
Bear Paw & Initials	**Del Fred Masawytewa** *Learned at the Guild. Brother of Darren Masawytewa.*	**Bear**	**Mishongnovi**	1991	
Bear Paw & Initials *G Masawytewa*	**Gary Masawytewa** *Learned at the Guild. Brother of Darren and Del Fred Masawytewa.*	**Bear**	**Mishongnovi**	1991	present
Sun's Forehead	**Ambrose Namoki** *Learned at the Guild.*	**Sun's Forehead**	**Shungopavi**	1991	
Sun's Forehead	**Merle Namoki** *Learned at the Guild. Nephew of Ambrose Namoki.*	**Sun's Forehead**	**Shungopavi**	1991	present
Bear Paw	**Aldrick Poleahla** *Learned at the Guild.*	**Bear**	**Shungopavi**	1991	present
Polequaptewa Winter Sun	**Alaric Polequaptewa** *Learned at the Guild. Son of Riley Polyquaptewa. Was working with Roy Talaheftewa in 1997.*	**Sun**	**Shungopavi**	1991	present
Masau	**Antoinette Qumawunu** *Learned at the Guild. Wife of Loren Qumawunu.*	**Masau**	**Kykotsmovi**	1991	
Parrot	**Darren Silas** *Learned at the Guild.*	**Parrot**	**Sichomovi**	1991	

HALLMARK	SILVERSMITH	CLAN	VILLAGE	BEGAN SILVER WORK	WORKED SILVER UNTIL
Sun's Rays	**Robert Puhyaoma Suqnevahya** *Learned at the the Guild.*	Sun's Forehead	**Shipaulovi**	1991	present
Cloud	**Belvin Yuyaheova** *Learned at the Guild.*	Snow	**Shungopavi**	1991	present
Lightning, Rain, Corn	**Lamar Barehand** *Learned at the Guild; nephew of Milland Lomakema.*	Corn	**Shungopavi**	1992	present
Bear used with Dawn 1994	**Fernando Batala** *Learned from wife, Dawn Lucas.*	Sun's Forehead	**Shipaulovi**	1992	present
Sun & Name	**Iva Casuse** *Learned on her own and from husband, Louie Hawk (Yakima).*	Sun	**Shungopavi**	1992	
Rabbit Track & Spider Web	**Brian Holmes** *Learned from his father, Emory Holmes.*	Spider	**Hotevilla**	1992	
Frog	**Ferron Joseyesva** *Learned at the Guild. Nephew of Gracilda Saufkie, stepson of Ross Joseyesva.*	Fog	**Shungopavi**	1992	present
EK	**Elroy Kewanyama** *Learned at the Guild.*	Strap	**Shungopavi**	1992	

HALLMARK	SILVERSMITH	CLAN	VILLAGE	BEGAN SILVER WORK	WORKED SILVER UNTIL
Bear Track/Initial	**Quinton Laban** *Learned from grandfather, Victor Coochwytewa.*	**Bear**	**Shungopavi**	1992	present
Sun's Face	**Palmer Lomakema** *Learned from uncle, Clifton Mowa.*	**Sun's Forehead**	**Mishongnovi**	1992	
Sun's Face	**Kendrick Lomayestewa** *Learned at the Guild. Son of Clarence Lomayestewa, brother of Lendrick.*	**Sun**	**Shungopavi**	1992	present
Rabbit & Name	**Harry Nutumya** *Learned from Loren Phillips.*	**Rabbit**	**Oraibi-Shipaulovi-Mishongnovi**	1992	present
D P	**Darrell Pooyouma** *Brother of Gene Pooyouma.*	**Sun's Forehead**	**Hotevilla**	1995	
Sun & Corn	**Gene Pooyouma** *Nephew of Allen Pooyama.*	**Sun's Forehead**	**Hotevilla**	1992	
PUHU-YAMA	**Darrell Taylor Puhuyama** *Learned at the Guild. Wayne Taylor's son.*	**Sun**	**Shungopavi**	1992	
Turtle	**Sidney Sahneyah** *Learned from Perry Fred, his brother.*	**Fog**	**Shungopavi**	1992	present
Initials	**Marsha Shupla** *Learned from Louie Joseytewa.*	**Sun's Forehead**	**Shungopavi**	1992	

HALLMARK	SILVERSMITH	CLAN	VILLAGE	BEGAN SILVER WORK	WORKED SILVER UNTIL
DT	**Duane Tawahongva** *Younger brother of Berra Tawahongva.*	**Coyote**	**Mishongnovi**	1992	
L	**Lewis Quiyo** *Brother-in-law is Bradley Gashwazra.*	**Eagle**	**Mishongnovi**	1992	
Initials	**Cordelia Casuse** *Learned from Wilson Mowa.*	**Sun**	**Shungopavi**	1993	present
Turtle (1996)	**Art Honani** *Brother of King Honani.*	**Fog**	**Shipaulovi**	1993	present
Cloud / Turtle	**Antone Honanie** *Learned from Guild.*	**Fog**	**Kykotsmovi**	1993	present
Initials	**Ernest W. Honanie** *Learned from Gary Yoyoki. Brother of Aaron Honanie.*	**Fog**	**Shungopavi-Kykotsmovi**	1990	
Turtle	**Hallie Honanie** *Learned from Lendrick Lomayestewa. Formerly used name Talayumptewa.*	**Fog**	**Kykotsmovi**	1993	present
HK	**Hale Kahe** *Learned at Honani Crafts.*	**Water Patki**	**Sichomovi**	1993	present

HALLMARK	SILVERSMITH	CLAN	VILLAGE	BEGAN SILVER WORK	WORKED SILVER UNTIL
Snowflakes	Ryan Kuyvaya *Steven Pooyouma Kuyvaya's son.*	Fog	Shungopavi	1993	
	Marshall Lomayaktewa *Learning from son, Moody Lomayaktewa. He is also a weaver.*	Spider	Mishongnovi	1993	
DS	Darrell Sakeva *Learned from his brother, Loren Qumawunu.*	Corn	Shungopavi	1993	
Masau & Initials	Lucinda Taylor *Learned from husband Milson Taylor.*	Masau	Kykotsmovi	1993	present
	Tyrone Honie *Learned from grandfather, Norman Honie.*	Fog	Shungopavi	1994	present
CM	Chris Mansfield *Learned from his father Verden Mansfield.*	Greasewood	Hotevilla	1994	killed 1996
Spider & Cloud	Fletchard Namingha *Learned from his brother Floyd Namingha.*	Strap	Shungopavi	1994	present
M.S. Corn Plant & Initials	Michele L. Sockyma *Learned from father Michael Sockyma, Sr.*	Bear	Kykotsmovi	1994	
Yowytewa	Faron Yowytewa *Uses initials or script name that was never used by his uncle Hubert. Learned from father Earl Yowytewa.*	Sand	Hotevilla	1994	
Rabbit	Roy Dawangyumptewa *Learned from Michael Sockyma, father-in-law.*	Rabbit	Sichomovi-Kykotsmovi	1995	present

HALLMARK	SILVERSMITH	CLAN	VILLAGE	BEGAN SILVER WORK	WORKED SILVER UNTIL
Cloud & Lightning	**Francis Harvey** *Loren Qumawunu's nephew. Learned at Guild.*	**Water Patki**	**Shungopavi**	**1995**	
Arrow	**Todd Hoyungwa** *Learned from father, Manuel Hoyungwa.*	**Water Patki**	**Hotevilla**	**1995**	
Triple Arrows	**Troy Hoyungwa** *Learned from father Manuel Hoyungwa, brother of Todd.*	**Water Patki**	**Hotevilla**	**1995**	**d. 2001**
BU-LEE Name	**Carol Humeyestewa** *Wife of Jay Humeyestewa.*	**Masau**	**Mishongnovi**	**1995**	**present**
Initial	**Mae Kinale** *Learned from Alvin Taylor.*	**Kachina**	**Tewa**	**1995**	
Initials	**Christine Kuwanvayouma** *Father is Kenneth Kuwanvoyouma.*	**Strap**	**Shungopavi**	**1995**	
Bear Paw	**Dorothy Ann Lucas** *Daughter of Glenn Lucas. Working in 1995.*	**Bear**	**Mishongnovi**	**1995**	
Initials	**Victor Lee Masayesva** *Cast work.*	**Snake**	**Bacavi**	**1993**	
Little Fox	**Lyman Nasawytewa** *Working in 1995.*	**Coyote-Fire**	**Bacavi**	**1995**	
Snowflake	**Monte Navasie** *Working in 1995.*	**Snow**	**First Mesa**	**1995**	
Corn	**Charles Wadsworth** *Learned from his father, Ted Wadsworth.*	**Corn**	**Shungopavi**	**1995**	

HALLMARK	SILVERSMITH	CLAN	VILLAGE	BEGAN SILVER WORK	WORKED SILVER UNTIL
Corn Plant	**Donald Wadsworth** *Learned from his father, Ted Wadsworth.*	**Corn**	**Shungopavi**	1995	
MY	**Marcus Yowyetewa** *Learned from father Earl Yowytewa.*	**Sand**	**Hotevilla**	1995	
1989 / SONWAI — / SH / 1993 / Butterfly 1997	**Sherian Honhongva** *Charles Loloma's niece and Verma Nequatewa's sister. Used Sonwai mark with Verma from 1989 to late 1993.*	**Badger**	**Hotevilla**	1983	**present**
New Mark 1994	**Gordon Honyestewa**	**Corn**	**Hotevilla Moenkopi**	1988	**present**
	Louie Josytewa *Brother of Jesse.*	**Snow**	**Shungopavi**	ca. 1985	
FK	**Lewis (Fabbie) Kagenvema** *Learned at the Guild. Son of Richard and brother of Bennett Kagenvema.*	**Strap**	**Shungopavi**	1991	**present**

GUILD HALLMARKS

HALLMARK	GUILD	LOCATION	BEGAN SILVER WORK	WORKED SILVER UNTIL
	Hopicrafts	**Kykotsmovi**	**1962**	**1983**
	Hopi silver shop owned by Wayne and Emory Sekaquaptewa. The business was first located in Phoenix and was called Hopi Enterprises. The workshop was later located at Kykotsmovi.			
	Kopavi International	**Sedona**	**1976**	
	A business owned by a non-Indian, Richard A. Mehagian, in Sedona, Arizona. He commissions Hopi silversmiths to make jewelry of both silver and gold of their own design as well as incorporating suggestions of his. Bell mark used on pieces during the Bicentennial, 1976.			
	Honani Crafts	**Second Mesa**		
	Shop at Winslow crossroads employing several smiths in 1988.			
	Shades of the West	**Scottsdale**		
	Scottsdale shop using mark on jewelry made by Indian craftsmen in their shop.			
	Charles Loloma Studio		**1996**	**present**
	Reproduction of Charles Loloma's work.			
See Below	**Hopi Silvercraft Guild**	**Second Mesa**	**1949**	**present**
	Each smith has his own Guild stamp. Consequently, none are exactly alike, as is shown in the few illustrated here. Mailing address is Second Mesa..			

INDEX OF HALLMARKS BY TYPE

ANIMALS

	Antelope— Arthur Allen Lomayestewa, p. 94		Bear— Travis Yaiva, p. 80		Coyote— Dewan Sumatzkuku, p. 80
	Antelope—Arthur Allen Lomayestewa, p. 94		Bear— Lawrence Saufkie, p. 77		Fox Ears and Fox— Art Batala, p. 89
	Antelope— Verden Mansfield, p. 89		Bear— Fernando Batala, p. 107		Little Fox— Lyman Nasawytewa, p. 111
	Antelope Head— Danny Kuwanvayouma, p. 100		Bear Claw— Marshall Jenkins, p. 77		Rabbit— Eldon James, p. 81
	Antelope Head— Dwayne Lomayestewa, p. 94		Bear Claw— Rosella Nutumya, p. 101		Rabbit— Mark Tawahongya, p. 96
	Antelope— Benjamin Mansfield, p. 95		Bear Fangs— Ronald Youvella, p. 89		Rabbit— Harry Nutumya, p. 108
	Antelope— Arlo Nuvayaouma, p. 84		Bear Paw— Dorothy Ann Lucas, p. 111		Rabbit—Roy Dawangyumptewa, p. 110
	Antelope Horn— Myron Secakuku, p. 90		Coyote Head— Grant Jenkins, p. 76		

ANIMAL TRACKS

	Bear Claws— Riley Polyquaptewa, p. 86		Bear Claws— Jay Humeyestewa, p. 91		Bear Paw— Del Fred Masawytewa, Tewa, p. 106
	Bear Claws— Riley Polyquaptewa, p. 86		Bear Paw— Alde Qumyintewa, p. 90		Bear Paw— Darren Masawytewa, p. 106
	Bear Paw— Ricky Coochwytewa, p. 84		Bear Paw— Philbert Poseyesva, p. 87		Bear Paw— Gary Masawytewa, p. 106
	Bear Paw— Marcus Coochwykvia, p. 85		Bear Paw— Philbert Poseyesva, p. 87		Bear Paw— Gary Masawytewa, p. 106
	Bear Paw— Watson Honanie, p. 87		Bear Paw— Orville Talayumptewa, p. 80		Bear Paw— Gerald Honwytewa, p. 98
	Bear Paw— Winfield Humeyestewa, p. 88		Bear Paw— Andrew Saufkie, p. 85		Bear Paw— Ila Lomawaima, p.105
	Bear Paw— Aldrick Poleahla, p. 106		Bear Paw—Jay Humeyestewa, p. 91		Antelope Track— Sidney Secakuku, Jr. p. 86
	Bear Paw— Quinton Laban, p. 108		Bear Paw— Malcorbin Lomakema, p. 100		Rabbit Track— Philbert Polingyouma, p. 90
	Bear Paw— Lambert Poseyesva, p. 100		Bear Paw— Willis Humeyestewa, p. 95		Rabbit Track— Fermin Hawee, p. 104
	Bear Paw— Elmer Setalla Jr., p. 103		Antelope Track— Ross Joseyesva, p. 85		Rabbit Track— Brian Holmes, p. 107

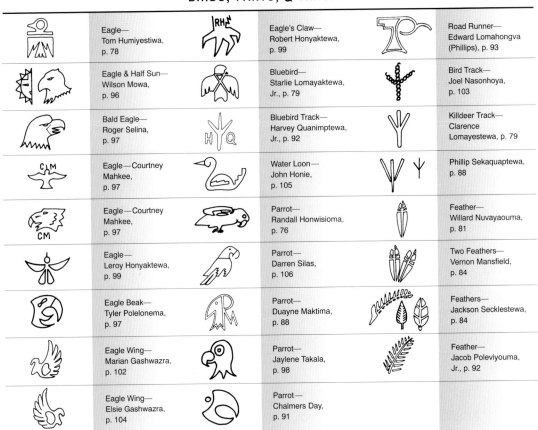

Eagle—Tom Humiyestiwa, p. 78	Eagle's Claw—Robert Honyaktewa, p. 99	Road Runner—Edward Lomahongva (Phillips), p. 93
Eagle & Half Sun—Wilson Mowa, p. 96	Bluebird—Starlie Lomayaktewa, Jr., p. 79	Bird Track—Joel Nasonhoya, p. 103
Bald Eagle—Roger Selina, p. 97	Bluebird Track—Harvey Quanimptewa, Jr., p. 92	Killdeer Track—Clarence Lomayestewa, p. 79
Eagle—Courtney Mahkee, p. 97	Water Loon—John Honie, p. 105	Phillip Sekaquaptewa, p. 88
Eagle—Courtney Mahkee, p. 97	Parrot—Randall Honwisioma, p. 76	Feather—Willard Nuvayaouma, p. 81
Eagle—Leroy Honyaktewa, p. 99	Parrot—Darren Silas, p. 106	Two Feathers—Vernon Mansfield, p. 84
Eagle Beak—Tyler Polelonema, p. 97	Parrot—Duayne Maktima, p. 88	Feathers—Jackson Secklestewa, p. 84
Eagle Wing—Marian Gashwazra, p. 102	Parrot—Jaylene Takala, p. 98	Feather—Jacob Poleviyouma, Jr., p. 92
Eagle Wing—Elsie Gashwazra, p. 104	Parrot—Chalmers Day, p. 91	

Snake Wand—Lawrence Koyayesva, p. 87	Kopituvuh, Breath of the Sun—Alvin Taylor, p. 104	Rabbit Stick—Ted Wadsworth, p. 80
Star Priest—Leroy Kewanyama, p. 80	Chief's Stick—Marcus Lomayestewa, p. 92	Rabbit Stick—Loren Phillips, p. 86
Star Priest—Harold Lomayaktewa, p. 97	Yaya's Rattle—Ernest Honyaktewa, p. 103	Rabbit Stick—Loren Phillips, p. 86
Peyote Bird—Preston Monongye, p. 77	Yaya's Rattle—Lucion Koinva, p 101	Rabbit Stick—Tony Kyasyousie, p. 86
Chief's Jug (Mong Wikoru)—Steven Pooyouma Kuyvaya, p. 89	Antelope Rattle—Charles T. Lomakima, p. 78	Rabbit Stick—Daniel Phillips, p. 84
Medicine Bowl—Steven Pooyouma Kuyvaya, p. 89	Rattle—Lauren Koinva, p. 87	Tree Stump—Duwayne Kopelva, p. 100
Chief's Jug—Willie Archie Talaheftewa Dawungnufti, p. 82	Antelope Rattle—Floyd Namingha Lomakuyvaya, p. 87	Crossed Arrows—Wallie Sekayumptewa, p. 79
One-Horn (Society)—Stewart Tewawina Dacawyma, p. 93	Antelope Rattle—Larry Humeyestewa, p. 98	George Phillips, p. 101
Flute Rattle—James Selina, p. 96	Flute—Marcus Lomayestewa, p. 92	Four Arrows—Gordon Honyestewa, p. 112
Lakon Corn—Ronald Wadsworth, p. 95	Pipe—Vernon Talas, p. 80	Triple Arrows—Troy Hoyungwa, p. 111
Nahsompi (Hair Whorl)—Edgar Miller Hovalo, p. 78	Pipe—Joe Coochyumptewa, p. 85	Arrow—Todd Hoyungwa, p. 111
Friendship Mark—Phillip Honanie, p. 83	Pipe—Roy Tawahongva, p. 86	Arrow and Initials—Nathan Fred Jr., p. 83
Lakon Rain Mark—Eddison Wadsworth Soohafyah, p. 97	Hook for Bear Strap—Jerry Honwytewa Whagado, p. 85	
Warrior Tracks—Larry Polivema, p. 87	Rabbit Stick—Ted Wadsworth, p. 80	

CLOUDS

Thundercloud & H (Hopi)—Ralph Tawangyaouma, p. 80	Cloud—Eldon Siwingyumptewa Kalemsa, p. 83	Cloud—Belvin Yuyaheova, p. 107	
Snow Cloud—Paul Saufkie, Sr., p. 80	Snow Cloud—Eldon Siwingyumptewa p. 83	Cloud & Pahos—Harlan Joseph, p. 101	
Thunderhead—Sidney Secakuku, Sr. p. 77	Snow Cloud—Bueford Dawahoya, p. 89	Snow Cloud—Fernando Puhuhefvaya, p. 102	
Rain Cloud—Victor Coochwytewa, p. 77	Strong Rain—Bueford Dawahoya, p. 89	Cloud & Corn—Charleston Lewis, p. 105	
Cloud—Dean Siwingyumptewa, p. 79	Strong Rain—Manuel Hoyungwa, p. 90	Lightning, Rain, Corn—Lamar Barehand, p. 107	
Snow Cloud—Mark Lomayestewa, p. 81	Snow Cloud—Manuel Hoyungva, p. 90	Cloud—Antone Honanie, p. 109	
Snow Cloud—Bernard Dawahoya, p. 81	Snow Cloud—Jason Takala, p. 83	Rain & Lightning—Ruben Saufkie, p. 100	
Snow Cloud 1965—Griselda Saufkie, p. 82	Snow Cloud—Jason Takala, p. 83	Cloud, Rain, & Lightning—Francis Harvey, p. 111	
Snow Cloud—Griselda Saufkie, p. 82	Snow Cloud—Jason Takala, p. 83	Cloud—William Lalo Lomawunu, p. 105	
Snowflake—Patrick Lomawaima, p. 82	Cloud—Pat Tewawina, p. 93	Snowflake, Cloud—Michael Selina, p. 99	
Cloud—Patrick Lomawaima, p. 82	Cloud—Chalmers Day, p. 91		
Snow Cloud—Manuel Poseyesva, p. 82	Rain Cloud—Emerson H. Quannie, p. 83		

FIGURES, KACHINAS

Masau-u—Willie Coin, p. 76	Masau-u—Antoinette Qumawunu, p. 106	War God—Cedric (Navenma) Kuwaninvaya, p. 92	
Masau-u & Initials—Lucinda Taylor, p. 110	War God—Cortez Lomahukva, p. 78	Masau-u—Berra Tawahongva, p. 96	

FIGURES, KACHINAS (continued)

	Crow Mother Howard Dennis, p. 104		Man— Alvin Sosolde, p. 86		Flute Player & Name— Don Supplee, p. 102
	Crow Mother— Bert Puhuyestiwa, p. 79		Man— Starlie Polacca III, p. 87		Carried in Beauty— Preston Duwyenie, p. 94
	Man's Head Scarf— Earl Numkina, p. 75		Flute Player— Pascal Nuvamsa Kuwanhongwa, p.98		Kachina— Unknown

FROGS & REPTILES

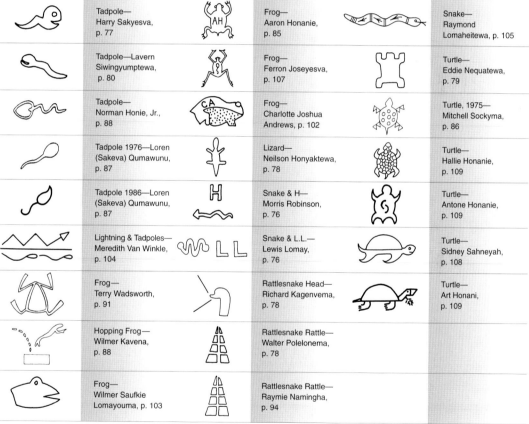

	Tadpole— Harry Sakyesva, p. 77		Frog— Aaron Honanie, p. 85		Snake— Raymond Lomaheitewa, p. 105
	Tadpole—Lavern Siwingyumptewa, p. 80		Frog— Ferron Joseyesva, p. 107		Turtle— Eddie Nequatewa, p. 79
	Tadpole— Norman Honie, Jr., p. 88		Frog— Charlotte Joshua Andrews, p. 102		Turtle, 1975— Mitchell Sockyma, p. 86
	Tadpole 1976—Loren (Sakeva) Qumawunu, p. 87		Lizard— Neilson Honyaktewa, p. 78		Turtle— Hallie Honanie, p. 109
	Tadpole 1986—Loren (Sakeva) Qumawunu, p. 87		Snake & H— Morris Robinson, p. 76		Turtle— Antone Honanie, p. 109
	Lightning & Tadpoles— Meredith Van Winkle, p. 104		Snake & L.L.— Lewis Lomay, p. 76		Turtle— Sidney Sahneyah, p. 108
	Frog— Terry Wadsworth, p. 91		Rattlesnake Head— Richard Kagenvema, p. 78		Turtle— Art Honani, p. 109
	Hopping Frog— Wilmer Kavena, p. 88		Rattlesnake Rattle— Walter Polelonema, p. 78		
	Frog— Wilmer Saufkie Lomayouma, p. 103		Rattlesnake Rattle— Raymie Namingha, p. 94		

Mark	Name	Mark	Name	Mark	Name
A	Art Batala, p. 89		Cordelia Casuse, p. 109		Bennard Dallasvuyaoma, p. 83
AB	Art Batala, p. 89		Caroline Fred (Mansfield), p. 104		Dawn Lucas, p. 98
AG	Alfonso Gashwazra, p. 89	CH	Clement Honie, p. 104	DL	Dawn Lucas, p. 98
AH	Anthony Honahnie, p. 88		Cleve Honyaktewa, p. 95	DM	Del Fred Masawytewa, p. 106
AH	Antone Honanie, p. 109	CK	Christine Kuwanvoyouma, p. 111		Daniel Phillips, p. 84
	Art Honani, p. 109	CM	Chris Mansfield, p. 110		Dorothy Poleyma Kyasyousie, p. 102
A Q	Antoinette Qumawunu, p. 106	CM	Courtney Mahkee, p. 97	Dp	Darrell Pooyouma, p. 108
AS	1974— Andrew Saufkie, p. 85	CM	Courtney Mahkee, p. 97	DS	Darrell Sakeva, p. 110
BG	Bradley Gashwazra, p. 81		Charles Supplee, p. 91		Darren Seweyestewa, p. 100
	Bryan Humeyestewa, p. 90		Courtney Amon Scott, p. 88		Doran Sehongva Puhudawa, p. 90
	Bryan Humeyestewa, p. 90		Charles Supplee, p. 91		Doran Sehongva Puhudawa, p. 90
	Bob Sekakuku, p. 86	CW	Cheryl Wadsworth Soohafyah, p. 96	DT	Duane Tawahongva, p. 109
BY	Belvin Yuyaheova, p. 107		Darren Seweyestewa, p. 101	EA	Everett Adams, p. 105
	Courtney Amon Scott, p. 88	DAL	Dorothy Ann Lucas, p. 111		Emery Holmes, p. 90

EJ	Eldon James, p. 81	FY	Faron Yowytewa, p. 111	HE	Ernest W. Honanie, p. 109
EK	Elroy Kewanyama, p. 107	G	Michael Gashwazra, p. 104	HE	Hopi Enterprises 1961, Hopi Crafts 1962, p. 113
☰	Eddie Scott, Jr., p. 92	MASA G	Gary Masawytewa, p. 104	JH	Harlan Joseph, p. 101
E^S	Eddie Scott, Jr., p. 92	*G Masawytewa*	Gary Masawytewa, p. 106	HK	Hale Kahe, p. 109
	Elgene Sehongva, p. 88	GH	Gordon Honyestewa, p. 112	H	Helena Lucas Namingha, p. 98
	Elgene Sehongva, p. 88	GL	Glenn Lucas, p. 83	HN	Stephen Hyson Naseyoma, p. 93
E. S.	Elmer Setalla, Jr., p. 103	GP	George Phillips, p. 101	HNL	Helena Lucas Namingha, p. 98
ESSIII	Eddie Scott, III, p. 102	G⋙⋙P	Grant Pawicki, p. 92	HT	Hubert Taylor, p. 91
F̄T	Effie Tawahongva Naquahyeoma, p. 101	GT	Gilbert Andress Tyma, p. 89	HY	Hubert Yowytewa, p. 82
E Y	Earl Yowytewa, p. 85	GY	Gary Yoyokie, p. 84	ᴵᴺL	Irvin Lomay, p. 97
EY	Elsie Yoyokie, p. 84	GY EY	Gary & Elsie Yoyokie, p. 84	JH	Jay Humayestewa, p. 91
FB	Fernando Batala, p. 107	H	Grant Jenkins, p. 76	J	Jay Humayestewa, p. 91
FK	Lewis (Fabbie) Kagenvema, p. 113	H	Eddison Wadsworth, p. 97	JF	Julian Fred, p. 104
FL ‡	Unknown, p. 113	H₀	Unknown, p. 113	J	Ferron Joseyesva, p. 112

Mark	Maker	Mark	Maker	Mark	Maker
J	Jesse Josewytewa, p. 94		Larry Pooyouma, p. 90		Merle Sehongva, p. 102
JwL	James Rawn Lomay, p. 98		Loren Phillips, p. 86	MS	Michael Sockyma, p. 82
JN	Unknown, p. 113		Loren Phillips, p. 86	MS	Mitchell Sockyma, p. 86
JYN	Jim Nutima, p. 85	LP	Loren Phillips, p. 86	MS	Mitchell Sockyma, p. 86
KT	Kevin Takala, p. 104	M	Mae Kinale, p. 111	Mt	Mark Tawahongva, p. 96
KT	Kevin Takala, p. 104	ML	Marcus Coochwykvia, p. 85	MY	Marcus Yowytewa, p. 112
L	Lewis Quiyo, p. 109	MG	Michael Gashwazra, p. 104	NF	Nathan Fred Jr., p. 83
LK	Lucion Koinva (1995), p. 100	MJ	Murray Jackson, p. 93	NR	Nathan Fred Jr., p. 83
LL	Lucy Lucas, p. 103	M	Marshall Lomayaktewa, p. 110	NF	Nathan Fred Jr., p. 83
LM	Loren Maha, p. 101	ML	Marvin Lucas Naquahyeoma (1990's), p. 95	NHJR	Norman Honie Jr., p. 88
LP	Lambert Poseyesva, p. 100	ML	Marvin Lucas Naquahyeoma, p. 95	NL	Nadine Lalo Lomawunu, p. 105
LP	Lambert Poseyesva, p. 100	MLK	Lucion Koinva (with wife), p. 101	NR	Raymie Namingha, p. 94
LP	Lambert Poseyesva, p. 100	MLK	Melinda Lucas Koinva (with husband), p. 105		Philbert Dennis, p. 88
LP	Larry Polivema, p. 87	M	Marsha Shupla, p. 108		Philbert Dennis, p. 88

P F	Perry Fred, p. 99	NL	Ryan Honyaktewa, p. 105	ᛋᛋ	Steven Sockyma, p. 84
ℙ F	Perry Fred & Petra Lamson, p. 99	R K	Raymond Kyasyousie, p. 91	B	Tony Anthony Burton, p. 101
ℙ	Loren Phillips, p. 86	R S	Randall Sahmie, p. 83	T H	Tyrone Honie, p. 110
P∿L	Peggy Lomay, p. 97	R T	Roy Tawahongva, p. 86	TK	Tony Kyasyousie, p. 84
PM	Preston Monongye, p. 77	S	Elmer Setalla, Jr., p. 103	T L d	Trinidad "Trini" Lucas, p. 94
ᑎᑎ	Philbert Poseyesva, p. 87	S H	Sherian Honhongva, p. 112	Y	Virgil Thomas, p. 86
ℙS	Phillip Sekaquaptewa, p. 88	ᛋN	Sharold Nutumya, p. 89	WV	Victor Masayesva, p. 111
R	Robert Puhuyaoma Suqnevahya, p. 107	ᛋP	Steven Pooyouma Kuyvaya, p. 89	WL	William Lalo Lomawunu, p. 105
R	Ramon (Albert, Jr.) Dalangyawma, p. 93	S P 3	Starlie Polacca III, p. 87		
RD	Reginald Dewakuku, p. 102	ᛋᛋ	Steven Sockyma, p. 84		

INSECTS & SPIDERS

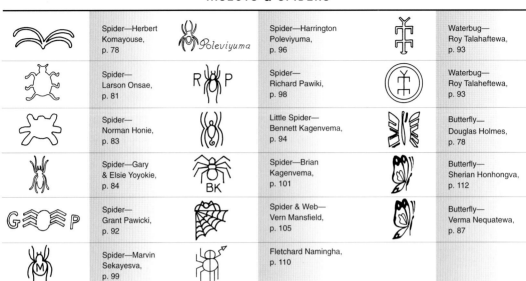

Spider—Herbert Komayouse, p. 78	Spider—Harrington Poleviyuma, p. 96	Waterbug—Roy Talahaftewa, p. 93
Spider—Larson Onsae, p. 81	Spider—Richard Pawiki, p. 98	Waterbug—Roy Talaheftewa, p. 93
Spider—Norman Honie, p. 83	Little Spider—Bennett Kagenvema, p. 94	Butterfly—Douglas Holmes, p. 78
Spider—Gary & Elsie Yoyokie, p. 84	Spider—Brian Kagenvema, p. 101	Butterfly—Sherian Honhongva, p. 112
Spider—Grant Pawicki, p. 92	Spider & Web—Vern Mansfield, p. 105	Butterfly—Verma Nequatewa, p. 87
Spider—Marvin Sekayesva, p. 99	Fletchard Namingha, p. 110	

PLANTS

Ear of Corn—Allen Pooyama, p. 77	Young Corn—Larry Pooyouma, p. 90	Squash—Kirkland Lomawaima, p. 79
Ear of Corn—Franklin Namingha, p. 84	Corn Plant—William Setalla, p. 91	Tobacco Leaf—Everett Harris, p. 77
Corn Plant—Michael Sockyma, p. 82	Corn Plant—Evanette Sockyma, p. 103	Tobacco Flower—Calvin Hastings, p. 77
Corn Plant, 1975—Michael Sockyma, p. 82	Corn Plant—Michele Sockyma, p. 110	Tobacco Leaf—Edgar Coin, p. 80
Corn Plant—Kenneth Kuwanvayouma, p. 84	Corn Plant—Michael C. Sockyma, Jr., p. 103	Tobacco Leaf—John Coochyumptewa, p. 91
Corn Ear—Raymond Sequaptewa, p. 85	Corn Kernels—Charles Wadsworth, p. 111	Waterbird, & Flute Flower—Philbert Selina, p. 99
Corn—Delbert Nevayaktewa, p. 92	Corn Plant—Donald Wadsworth, p. 112	Unknown p. 113

STARS & MOON

Crescent Moon—Valjean Joshevema, Sr., p. 78	Star—Dalton Taylor, p. 85	Star & Moon—Stetson Lomayestewa, p. 95	
Star—Harold Koruh, p. 78	Star—Terrance Lomayestewa, p. 95	Sun, Star, & Moon—Augustine Mowa, Jr., p. 95	
Star & Crescent Moon—Billie Ray Hawee, p. 81	Star—Terrance Lomayestewa, p. 95	Unknown	
Orion—Vernon Mansfield, p. 81	Shooting Star—Lendrick Lomayestewa, p. 95	Unknown	

SUN

Sun—Samuel N. Laban, p. 78	Sun—Roderick Phillips, p. 86	Sun's Mouth—Tim Mowa, p. 96	
Sun—Arthur Yowytewa, p. 81	Sun's Face—Kendrick Lomayestewa, p. 108	Sun's Forehead—Henry Polingyouma, p. 79	
Sun—Hubert Yowytewa, p. 82	Winter Sun—Alaric Polequaptewa, p. 106	Sun's Forehead—Weaver Selina, p. 83	
Sun—Larry Polivema, p. 87	Sun—Palmer Lomakewa, p. 108	Sun's Forehead—Delmar Lamson, p. 97	
Sun & Corn Plant—Gene Pooyouma, p. 108	Sun—Palmer Lomakewa, p. 108	Sun's Forehead—Jack Nequatewa, p. 100	
Sun Face—Charles Supplee, p. 91	Sun—Greg Naseyouma, p. 103	Sun's Forehead—Edward Nequatewa, p. 98	
Sun Face—Charles Supplee, p. 91	Sun Face—Iva Casuse, p. 107	Sun's Forehead—Merle Namoki, p. 106	
Sun—Milson Taylor, p. 93	Sun Face—Moody Lomayaktewa, p. 97	Sun's Forehead—Melson Harris, p. 102	
Sun—Milson Taylor, p. 93	Sun—Fernanda Lomayestewa, p. 94	Sun's Forehead—Michael Harris, p. 103	

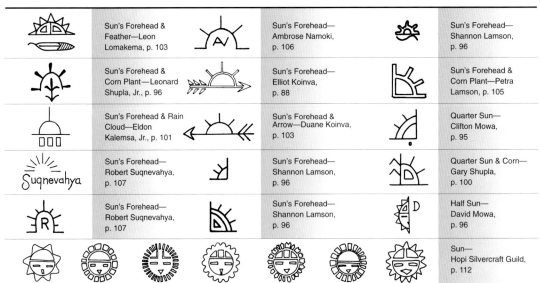

Sun's Forehead & Feather—Leon Lomakema, p. 103	Sun's Forehead—Ambrose Namoki, p. 106	Sun's Forehead—Shannon Lamson, p. 96
Sun's Forehead & Corn Plant—Leonard Shupla, Jr., p. 96	Sun's Forehead—Elliot Koinva, p. 88	Sun's Forehead & Corn Plant—Petra Lamson, p. 105
Sun's Forehead & Rain Cloud—Eldon Kalemsa, Jr., p. 101	Sun's Forehead & Arrow—Duane Koinva, p. 103	Quarter Sun—Clifton Mowa, p. 95
Sun's Forehead—Robert Suqnevahya, p. 107	Sun's Forehead—Shannon Lamson, p. 96	Quarter Sun & Corn—Gary Shupla, p. 100
Sun's Forehead—Robert Suqnevahya, p. 107	Sun's Forehead—Shannon Lamson, p. 96	Half Sun—David Mowa, p. 96
		Sun—Hopi Silvercraft Guild, p. 112

WEATHER

Snowflake, 1965—Patrick Lomawaima, p. 82	Snow Flake—Philbert Selina, p. 99	Lightning—McBride Lomayestewa, p. 81
Snowflake—Jesse Josewytewa, p. 94	Snow Flake—Jayme Takala (Nuva-lawu), p. 102	Lightning & Spider—Marvin Lomaheftewa, p. 92
Snowflake—Jesse Josytewa, p. 94	Snowballs—Vinton Selina, p. 99	Rainbow—Maynard Talaheftewa, p. 101
Snowflake—Guy Josytewa, p. 100	Snowballs—Vinton Selina, p. 99	Joe Josytewa, p. 100
Snowflake—Monte Navasie, p. 112	Snowman—Cyrus Josytewa, Jr., p. 99	
Snowflakes—Ryan Kuyvaya, p. 110	Lightning—Dawson Numkina, p. 79	

I

APPENDIX

Working silversmiths listed by John Adair in 1938:

Adair 1946, p. 194–195

AT MOENKOPI:
Harold Jenkins
Earl Numkina
Frank Nutaima

AT HOTEVILLA:
Sakwiam
Katchioma
Jean Nivawhioma
Titus Lamson
Dan Kwiamawioma

AT BAKAVI:
Willie Coin

AT SHONGOPOVI:
Paul Saufkie
Washington Talaiumtewa

AT SICHOMOVI:
Roscoe Narvasi

OUTSIDE THE RESERVATION:
Ralph Tawagioma, of Hotevilla, works
in Phoenix
Bert Frederick, of Oraibi, works in Flagstaff
Pierce Kewaytewa, of Oraibi, works
in the pueblo at Zia
Homer Vance, of Shipaulovi, works
at Williams
Randall Honowisioma, of Mishongnovi,
works at Williams

Working silversmiths listed by Mary-Russell F. in 1939:

Plateau 12, p. 7

Bert Frederick
Randal Honwisioma
Pierce Kewanwytewa
Dan Koitshongva
Titus Lamson
Lewis Lomayesva
Harry A. Nosewytewa
Earl Numkina

Frank Nutaima
Jean Nuvahoyowma
Morris Robinson
Sakhoioma
Paul Sifki
Washington Talaiumptewa
Ralph Tawangyawma
Homer Vance

Note the difference in spelling the names of the smiths. This is common when attempts are made by researchers to spell Indian names in English.

II

APPENDIX

STANDARDS FOR NAVAJO, PUEBLO, AND HOPI SILVER

In announcing its standards for the Government mark for Navajo, Pueblo, and Hopi silver and turquoise products, the Indian Arts and Crafts Board makes the following statement:

Navajo, Hopi, and Pueblo silverwork, as an art and as a product with a "quality" market, has been overwhelmed by machine production. The Indian craftsman, struggling to compete in price with the machine-made and factory-made imitations, has in turn been forced to adopt a machine technique, while at the same time his wages or earnings have been depressed to the "sweat-shop" level. Quality has been sacrificed to that extreme where Indian jewelry has become hardly more than a curio or souvenir.

There is being produced, though in relatively small quantity, Indian silver and turquoise work as fine as ever produced in the older days. And there are many Indian craftsmen who, if a quality market can be restored, will eagerly and capably produce work as good as the best of earlier times.

They cannot, however, produce it in price competition with factory output, machine output, and "bench-work" semi-machine output.

The Arts and Crafts Board has studied the situation thoroughly and has sought the counsel of Indians, of Indian traders, and of specialists in the marketing of craft products. The Board has reached the conclusion that the Government mark should be applied only to the finest quality of wholly genuine, truly hand-fashioned, and authentic Indian silver and turquoise products.

Use of the Government mark is not obligatory on any Indian, any factory, or any merchant. The Board has no power or purpose to forbid such production by time-saving methods and with machine stereotyped and stinted materials as now supplies the curio market. But for the production which is worthy of a fine Indian tradition, the Board will make available the Government certificate of genuineness and of quality; and the Board will seek to widen the existing "quality" market and to find new markets for such output as deserves the Government mark. In the measure of its success, the Board will help to bring about a larger reward for a greater number of Indian craftsmen, and to save from destruction a noble, historic art, which under right conditions can have a long future.

John Collier, *Chairman*
Indian Arts and Crafts Board
United States Department of Interior
Washington, D.C

Standards for Navajo, Pueblo, and Hopi Silver and Turquoise Products

Subject to the detailed requirements that follow, the Government stamp shall be affixed only to work individually produced and to work entirely hand-made. No object produced under conditions resembling a bench-work system, and no object in whose manufacture any power-driven machinery has been used, shall be eligible for the use of the Government stamp.

In detail, Indian silver objects, to merit the Government stamp of genuineness, must meet the following specifications:

(1) Material—Silver slugs of 1 ounce weight or other silver objects may be used, provided their fineness is at least 900; and provided further, that no silver sheet shall be used. Unless cast, the slug or other object is to be hand hammered to thickness and shape desired. The only exceptions here are pins or brooches or similar objects; ear screws for ear rings; backs for tie clasps and chain, which may be of silver of different fineness and mechanically made.

(2) Dies—Dies used are to be entirely hand-made, with no tool more mechanical than hand tools and vise. Dies shall contain only a single element of the design.

(3) Application of dies—Dies are to be applied to the object with the aid of nothing except hand tools.

(4) Applique elements in design—All such parts of the ornament are to be hand-made. If wire is used, it is to be hand-made with no tool other than a hand-made draw plate. These requirements apply to the boxes for stone used in the design.

(5) Stone for ornamentation—In addition to turquoise, the use of other local stone is permitted. Turquoise, if used, must

be genuine stone, uncolored by any artificial means.

(6) Cutting of stone—All stone used, including turquoise, is to
be handcut and polished. This permits the use of hand- or
foot-driven wheels.

(7) Finish—All silver is to be hand polished.

For the present the Arts and Crafts Board reserves to itself the sole right
to determine what silver, complying with the official standards, shall be
stamped with the Government mark.

John Collier, *Chairman*   Harold L. Ickes,
                                                   Secretary of the Interior.

Approved March 9, 1937

"Gasoline and acetylene torches are permitted, since any industrious smith
can acquire one, and their use does not in any way affect the quality or
appearance of the finished product."

Kenneth M. Chapman
Special Consultant in Indian
Arts and Crafts

GLOSSARY

Anazi—Prehistoric Pueblo Indians of northern Arizona and New Mexico.

Anneal—To free the silver metal from internal stress by heating and gradual cooling. This permits the silver to shaped without cracking.

Bola tie—An ornament of silver, stone, or other material fastened onto a braided leather loop so that it slides up under the chin, leaving the two leather ends hanging, in place of a tie.

Bow guard—Wide leather strap worn on the left wrist, formerly to protect the arm from the bowstring. Usually decorated with a wide ornament of silver.

Concha—Spanish term for shell. One of the ovals of a segmented silver belt or of a bridle. Also the belt itself. Now commonly called concho.

Flatter—One type of a large double-headed blacksmith's hammer that is flat on one side and pointed on the other.

Flux—A substance applied to surfaces to be soldered which frees them from oxides so that they may be joined and will adhere.

Hohokam—Prehistoric Indians who lived in central and southern Arizona and made characteristic red-on-buff pottery.

Ingot—A mass of metal cast in some convenient shape for storage or for use.

Kachina—A Hopi supernatural being who may be impersonated by masked men or represented by a carved doll.

Kikmongwi—Hopi village chief.

Manta—Spanish term for coarse cotton cloth. As now used by the Hopi, it refers to the handwoven black woolen square used as a dress.

Maponi—Hopi name for bow guard. The Navajo word is ga-to or ke-toh.

Masau—One of the Hopi chief kachinas. In one of his aspects he is a deity of the underworld.

Matte or matting—The black background of Hopi overlay silver, as well as the process of texturing this background with a small chisel or die.

Mimbres—Prehistoric Indian group of southwestern New Mexico, noted for their black and white pottery, often with life forms.

Nahsompi—Stylized hair knot used as a distinguishing feature on some warrior kachinas.

Nukwivi—Hopi hominy stew.

Piki bread—A paper-thin wafer bread made by the Hopi from corn flour, especially blue corn.

Repoussé—Decoration formed by a raised pattern beaten up from the reverse side.

Squash blossom necklace—A necklace composed of a large center pendant and eccentric beads placed at regular intervals among the round beads on either side of the center. The eccentric beads often have three or four petals on them and are called squash blossoms.

Template—A cut-out metal pattern used to trace the design onto the silver overlay piece.

BIBLIOGRAPHY

Adair, John. *The Navajo and Pueblo Silversmiths.* Norman: University of
    Oklahoma Press, 1944.

Arizona Sun. Flagstaff: July 22, 1946.

Bahti, Tom. *Southwestern Indian Arts & Crafts.* Flagstaff: K. C. Publications, 1966.

Bartlett, Katharine. "Notes on the Indian Crafts of Northern Arizona." *Museum Notes*
    10:22–24. Flagstaff: Museum of Northern Arizona, 1938.

Bedinger, Margery. *Navajo Indian Silver Work.* Old West Series of Pamphlets, no. 8. Denver:
    John Van Male, 1936.

Colton, Harold S. "Exhibitions of Indian Arts and Crafts." *Plateau* 12:60–65. Flagstaff:
    Museum of Northern Arizona, 1940.

Colton, Mary-Russell F. "Hopi Silversmithing—Its Background and Future." *Plateau*
    12:1–7. Flagstaff: Museum of Northern Arizona, 1939.

Education Division, U.S. Indian Service. *Indian Education.* Jan. 15, 1949, p. 8.
    Washington, D.C.

Hodge, F. W. "How Old is Southwestern Indian Silverwork?" *El Palacio* 25:224–232.
    Santa Fe: Museum of New Mexico, 1928.

Kabotie, Fred. *Designs from the Ancient Mimbreños with a Hopi Interpretation.* San Francisco:
    Grabhorn Press, 1949.

———. *Hopi Silver.* Mimeographed catalog. Oraibi, Arizona: Hopi Silvercraft Guild, 1950.

McGibbeny, J. H. "Hopi Jewelry." *Arizona Highways* July 1950, pp. 18–25.

Mera, Harry P. *Indian Silverwork of the Southwest.* Vol. 1. Globe, Arizona: Dale Stuart King,
    1959.

Monongye, Preston. "The New Indian Jewelry Art of the Southwest." *Arizona Highways*
    June 1972, pp. 7–10.

Nequatewa, Edmund. *Truth of a Hopi*. Flagstaff: Museum of Northern Arizona, Bulletin 8 (1936; reprint ed. 1967).

Plateau. "Dr. Harold Sellers Colton 1881–1970." 43:146–147. Flagstaff: Museum of Northern Arizona, 1971.

Plateau. "Mary-Russell Ferrell Colton 1889–1971." 44:38–40. Flagstaff: Museum of Northern Arizona, 1971.

Ritzenthaler, Robert E. "Hopi Indian Silverwork." *Lore* 16:92–98. Milwaukee: Milwaukee Public Museum, 1966.

Indian Arts and Crafts Board, Dept. of Interior. *Smoke Signals*. Feb. 1963, p. 10. Washington, D.C.

Stephens, Alexander M. *Hopi Journal*. Edited by Elsie Crews Parsons, 2 vols. New York: Columbia University Press, 1936.

Stevenson, James. *Illustrated Catalogue of the Collections Obtained from the Indians of New Mexico and Arizona in 1879*. Second Annual Report 1880–1881, Smithsonian Institution. Washington, D.C.: Publications of the Bureau of Ethnology, 1883.

———. *Illustrated Catalogue of the Collections Obtained from the Pueblos of Zuñi, New Mexico, and Wolpi, Arizona in 1881*. Third Annual Report 1881–1882, Smithsonian Institution. Washington, D.C.: Publications of the Bureau of Ethnology, 1884.

Tanner, Clara Lee. "Contemporary Southwest Indian Silver." *Kiva* 25, no. 3, pp. 1–22. Tucson: Arizona State Museum, 1960.

———. "Crafts of Arizona Indians." *Arizona Highways* July 1960, pp. 8–35.

———. *Southwest Indian Craft Arts*. Tucson: University of Arizona Press, 1968.

Thompson, Laura and Joseph, Alice. *The Hopi Way*. 2nd ed. Chicago: University of Chicago Press, 1947.

Titiev, Mischa. *Old Oraibi, A Study of the Hopi Indians of Third Mesa*. Papers of the Peabody Museum of American Archaeology and Ethnology, vol. 22, no. 1. Cambridge: Peabody Museum, 1944.

Underhill, Ruth. *Here Come the Navajo*. Haskell, Kansas: United States Indian Service, 1953.

Whiting, Alfred F. *Hopi Arts and Crafts Survey for the Indian Arts and Crafts Board*. 4 vols. Flagstaff: Museum of Northern Arizona Archives, 1942.

Woodward, Arthur. *Navajo Silver: A Brief History of Navajo Silversmithing*. 1938. New ed. Flagstaff: Northland Press, 1971.

Wright, Barton A. "The Role of Tradition in Indian Crafts." *Tenth Scottsdale National Indian Arts Exhibition Catalog*, 1971, pp. 14–15.

GENERAL INDEX

INDEX OF ARTISTS

Born in LaJara, Colorado, MARGARET NICKELSON WRIGHT attended Adams State College in Alamosa; she later did postgraduate work at the University of Arizona. Margaret's knowledge of Hopi silverwork began with her twenty-two-year career at the Museum of Northern Arizona in Flagstaff, assisting curators and working with Hopi arts and crafts. She and her husband, Barton Wright, live in Phoenix.